Other Days Around Me

Other Days Around Me

ROBERT E. TANGNEY

BRANDON

To "Danny", Frank and Gerald, with thanks for the memories.

First published in 1989 by Brandon Book Publishers Ltd
Dingle, Co. Kerry, Ireland.

British Library Cataloguing in Publication Data
Tangney, Robert E.
  Other days around me.
  1. (Republic) Ireland. Urban regions. Social life, 1922-1949.
  Biographies
  I. Title
  941.7082'2'0924

ISBN 0-86322-107-6

Cover design by The Graphiconies, Dublin
Typeset by Koinonia Ltd, Manchester
Printed by Richard Clay Ltd, Bungay

Contents

Pennies from Heaven

I T WAS THE weeping and wailing that restored me to consciousness. I opened my eyes to discover that I was sharing a bed with a complete stranger. He was a little lad of about my own age and he was busily screaming his head off. I didn't have a clue as to what was bothering him, and having troubles enough of my own I cared little. If he was feeling as sickly as I was at that moment then he had good reason to cry, and as soon as I got my lungs primed I joined in to make it a duet. Side by side between the red-stained sheets we lay and keened our lamentations to the world.

It was the children's ward of the local infirmary and I had just come out of an ether-induced stupor; only four years on the road and I was in for overhaul and repair. My mother's story was that God had made me; that He had taken me from His workshop and given me to the good doctor Coffey, who in turn had brought me to our house in his little black bag. She said she had paid good money for me and thought she had got a bargain; I reckoned she had been fiddled. She had trouble with me from the beginning and was to go on having trouble with me. It was touch and go whether I would ever reach puberty such was my construction and constitution. Had it not been for her dedication, care and absolute faith in the health-giving properties of cod-liver oil I might never have lived to tell my tale.

I was the first of three children that my mother was lumbered with. The two later arrivals came our way more or less by accident; one could say they just dropped in. In those distant days the business of middle-man was not the exclusive prerogative of the family doctor: the stork held a large though diminishing slice of the baby market and I had heard it said that the postman carried more than letters in his sack. Though still a well-favoured supplier Mr Stork was losing his grip in more ways than one. Slip-shod delivery was leading to his early demise as a baby-monger and was also to result in my acquisition of a sister and brother.

My sister was found beneath a gooseberry bush, a victim of negligence or indifference on the part of one of these feathered traffickers. The shock of the fall coupled with the rough reception she received from the bush had a detrimental effect on her personality; a cry-baby, her screaming was so incessant that my father developed a nervous tic as a result. So bad did the situation become that two years later, when my mother came in from the garden carrying a cabbage under one arm and a new brother under the other, the Old Man threatened to run away from home and join the French Foreign Legion.

For children of such diverse origins we nevertheless managed to strike up a fairly reasonable relationship. Peace and harmony did not reign supreme at all times though. We did have our differences – they could perhaps be called wars – with innumerable alliances, treaties and pacts. My brother and I might sometimes be allies in a confrontation that would see our sister on the receiving end of a fist; a secret peace conference between the other two and then I would be the victim of an unprovoked two-pronged attack. The younger brother would at times get his come-uppance from two staunch and ever-loyal confederates. In a nutshell, we behaved very much like statesmen and politicians the world over.

PENNIES FROM HEAVEN

There were drawbacks in being the oldest of the children but there were some bonuses as well and one of these was being the first to come on to salary. Saturday was pay-day, and when the dad came in from work just after one o'clock he always presented me with the brightest penny that he could find among his small change. It was mine to spend as I desired. Wealth brings its problems and mine was decision making. Our local huckster, Micky Mac, waited patiently behind his little counter while I tried to make up my mind on how to dispose of my fortune. Should I blow the lot in one go? Should I save some for a rainy day? The serried ranks of glass jars lining his shelves never failed to boggle me. The bull's eyes, bonbons and Peggy's leg vied with the liquorice, sherbet and chocolates in their bid to part me from my dough. A born gambler, after long deliberation I would usually plump for a ha'penny money ball. With luck I might find a new ha'penny wrapped in grease-proof paper within this confection; a classic case of having one's cake after eating it.

As much as I looked forward to Saturday the strain it imposed on me at Micky's counter could have wreaked havoc on my nervous system had it not been for the intervention of the good Lord Himself. I discovered that I was the recipient of pennies from Heaven: the Almighty was hiding coins in the drawer of our hall-stand. I couldn't for the life of me figure out why someone else might do such a thing. I reckoned that He had me singled out for sainthood, or else I was earmarked as a future pope and was being put through a test. Whatever His plans for me were I had no intention of disappointing Him. I resolved not to succumb to the temptation dangled before me. Only a fool would kill the goose that was laying the golden eggs and I was no fool, so I limited my take to a maximum of one per day.

For months I conducted myself as behove a future bigwig of the church, enjoying my stipend and all the goodies that it bought. Convinced that for little more than walking the straight and narrow this divine beneficence was for life, I was almost devastated when I found myself suddenly abandoned by my celestial patron. I could never understand why I was so shamefully treated, though I did have my suspicions. It may have been mere coincidence, but I felt that He had been upset by those men from the gas company because, from the day that they came to remove the meter from behind the hall door, I never found another penny in that drawer.

Luckily I found an outside interest that took my mind off my deprivation and prevented me from wallowing in bouts of self-pity: I became a member of the gang. The "gang" was a living entity that reached out, drew me within, digested and transformed me into one of its pulsating cells. It was in a constant state of flux as new members were absorbed and older ones faded out. It had always been and always would be; it would grow or shrink but never die. Its only weakness lay in its members' intimate relationship with one another, rendering us susceptible to every contagious malady that stalked the land. The first one to pick up a dose of measles generously passed it around before taking to his bed; it was likewise with all other ailments. This propensity to share owed more to selfishness than selflessness; after all, who wanted to lie in bed counting spots or making with the whoop while the pals were outside the window making whoopee?

If the gang had what could be called headquarters they were to be found beneath the old gas-lamp that surmounted the green, grooved and gnarled cast-iron post that stood stoically on the pavement edge outside Frank's house. Of an evening as darkness crept in it held a more powerful influence over us than the Pied Piper's piccolo had held over the kids of Hamelin. It was our parliament, where we sat and discussed the events of the day and the woes of the world; it was our trading post, where we brought our frayed and grubby literature, exchanging the adventures of Eggo the Ostrich for a new episode in the exploits of Korky the Cat, where Kitty the Hare's tales of her weird wanderings could be swapped for another saga of Strang the Terrible. It served as our maypole and as a support for our swing. On autumn evenings its halo of yellow light outlined the arena in which fierce battles were fought to decide who owned the champion chestnut of the season.

When those men from the gas company whom I already suspected of being responsible for the termination of my lucrative financial arrangement with Himself came to remove our friend in the name of progress they committed an act of vandalism we could not easily forget. Although we were compensated for our loss with a brighter, more efficient electric lamp, it was aloof and impersonal, lacking the friendly, warm glow of its predecessor. The gaslight, though feeble, had embraced and protected us from the shadows of the night, imparting a feeling of cosy well-being. Now it was gone forever, leaving us to bear witness to the passing of an era.

Huddled together around our new lamppost, to a passing stranger we could easily be mistaken for homeless waifs. In tattered jerseys with holed elbows, our anaemic socks sagged limply upon mud-encrusted shoes and grubby knees peeped from beneath our frayed and multipatched trousers. Ignoring the gravity-defying pear-drops clinging doggedly to our nose ends, we were engrossed in deep discussion on "the coming". It was Christmas Eve and soon we would be hanging up stockings in anticipation of yet another visitation from that friend and benefactor to children everywhere – Santa Claus. As we informed each other of our expectations we knew full well that we were giving air to pipe-dreams and we were also aware that what we were hearing in return were figments of wishful imaginings. Every Christmas Eve before parting company we would exchange solemn promises to lay awake and surprise the Old Boy on his nocturnal ramblings, but it was never to be. We were always foiled in our ambitions by the earlier arrival of Mister Sandman, a shadowy character whose only purpose in life was to send children to sleep so that Santa could proceed about his business unhindered.

On Christmas morning before the crack of dawn every house on our street would reverberate with the delighted cries of children rummaging through their presents. After a hurried breakfast we would spill out onto the street in our urgency to show one and all what the grand Old Man had brought, and we were equally curious to see what he had deposited in other stockings. Old was the operative word when describing Santa. We had long since concluded that he was senile and over the hill, that he should apply for his pension and hand over the reins to his next-of-kin. He was out of touch with the modern world, completely devoid of imagination and severely limited in what he toted around in his old sack. Its contents never varied. Every year the street was thronged with cowboys, indians and New York cops. Still, to give credit where it was due, he never gave any lad a similar outfit two years running. This year's cowboy would almost certainly be biting the dust as a redskin next year. The cop wandering around with a pair of handcuffs in his grasp on the lookout for an escaped con would surely be attired for riding the range next time round. Mothers expressed no surprise on seeing Hopalong Cassidy leave the breakfast table and Sitting Bull, complete with war bonnet, arrive for Christmas dinner. No matter what one received it was never as good as the other fellow's, and we might even arrive for tea in a third rig-out. A consequence of all this swapping and changing was that within a few days all the costumes would disintegrate into rags and tatters. The only reminder that Santa had ever been would be a few clapped-out six-shooters, and these too would soon vanish like the snows of winter.

Tonight beneath the street light our discussions embraced not only the forthcoming visit and the benevolence of the visitor, but the question of his very existence. We knew in our hearts that at least one of our number would wake up in the morning to find that he had been overlooked by the old gent; that somewhere a stocking would hang limp and empty, and the victim of the oversight would no longer be one of us. He would in a few short hours be an unbeliever who would chide the others for their gullibility, and be among the most vociferous in condemnation of those who lacked the common sense to realise that there was no such person as Santa Claus. This change in attitude occurred so frequently, so suddenly and dramatically, that it became a problem that had to be resolved because it seemed certain that sooner or later we would all suffer the same fate. To our minds there had to be a logical explanation as to why Santa was a reality in early life and, overnight, gave up the ghost to descend into the realm of the fairy-tale.

The night's cold had penetrated to our bones before we were satisfied that the mystery was solved. There was not just one Santa, there were many: we each had our own. Just as each of us came into the world with a Guardian Angel so we had bestowed upon us a Santa Claus. There was one big difference between the two: our Guardian Angel remained by our sides throughout our lifetimes but our Santa was mortal, aged rapidly and expired while we were still in our childhood. We had stumbled upon a profound truth that filled us with sadness, but was more acceptable than to be told suddenly and bluntly that he had never really existed and that all we had been led to believe were the devil's lies. As we parted company and turned towards home I was struck by a sense of foreboding; I was overwhelmed with a fear of impending loss: I felt that my Santa had reached the end of his days.

Preparing for bed I put on a brave show and said nothing to betray my feelings to my sister and younger brother – their spirits were bubbling in innocent expectation. Their faith brushed off on me and raised faint hopes that my Santa was made of sterner stuff than the others' and might conceivably live longer than theirs.

I was roused by the delighted cries of the younger ones as they unwrapped the contents of their stockings. I lay and watched as my sister lovingly cradled her new doll and my brother fumbled awkwardly with the pin on his sheriff's badge. They were too engrossed in their own good fortune to notice me crawl gingerly to the foot of the bed. I peeped over the edge in fervent hope, but found myself confronted with abject disappointment. I had reached a watershed in life; it would never be the same again. My Father Christmas had passed away.

Crazy Horse

THOSE WERE THE days in which Ireland was a land of peace, if not of plenty. Here we were, the first generation of a young and free nation. Young it certainly was, but to call it free was from our point of view incredible. Where was this freedom we heard so much about? We could see no evidence of this wonderful quality of life that our forefathers had fought and died for. We were no freer than the galley slaves of yore. Dragged out of a warm, comfortable bed first thing in the morning while still in the throes of utter exhaustion, our sick stomachs, headaches and other sudden illnesses would bring forth ignominious charges of laziness and malingering, and do nothing to save us from being packed off to school to suffer the indignities of having useless information knocked into our heads by tyrannical teachers. Afternoons would see us reeling home, knees buckling under the weight of homework specifically compiled to reduce our funtime to an absolute minimum. Finally, in the evening, when getting into the swing of enjoying life, we were ordered to bed, all pleas and entreaties overruled. Those for whom life was a bed of roses had certainly off-loaded the thorns in our direction.

"You do as I say."

"No, you are not going out."

"And wash behind your ears."

There was no doubt about it, it was a hard life.

Complaints fell on deaf ears. To our elders and betters ours was an Arcadian idyll compared to their own youths back in the Dark Ages. That millions were suffering untold miseries throughout the world was a fact of which we were constantly and emphatically reminded. Such gems of knowledge were but poor consolation and did nothing to help sow seeds of solicitousness within our hearts. If people were stupid enough to live in foreign countries then they deserved what they got. We were already doing our best for them; we prayed regularly for the salvation of their souls when hunger and disease took them over the Great Divide. What more could be asked of us? A financial contribution towards the relief of those unfortunates' sufferings was definitely out of the question. The collection box on the sweet-shop counter silently pleading for a mite for the Black Babies vied in vain with the candy for our pennies. Sucking a lollipop we could walk out of the shop with clear consciences, knowing in our hearts that their travails would soon be at an end. A saviour had arisen.

The great Mussolini, who was the inspiration for our number one pop song, "Will You Come to Abyssinia", had already despatched his missionary men to the dark continent to bring to the savage the benefits of white civilization. The poor reception these good men had received added confirmation to our belief that our pennies were better spent on our own gratification. Whether they accepted their salvation or not was their affair; we had our own problems and cared not a whit. There were signs on the horizon that augured well for our own future well-being. In Germany a certain Mrs Hitler's little lad had thrown in the towel in his struggle to become a latter-day Michaelangelo and had started out on a crusade to avenge the Crucifixion and to rid the world of Jewry, which promised to be a fine example of killing two birds with one stone. Things were certainly looking up; a bright new world was on the way. There was only one cloud threatening to darken our seemingly bright future – Communism. Russia was the cradle from which this godless and unpleasant young baby had emerged. Its adolescence had been spent in the production of salt somewhere in the remoteness of Siberia, and now that it had reached maturity was seeking new territories into which it could stretch its bloodstained tentacles. It found in Spain a sun-kissed, poverty stricken victim for its first tentative step on the road to world domination. It could not have chosen a more formidable testing ground. The spirit of the old conquistadors still dwelt in the hearts of the indomitable Spaniards. The people of a land that had fostered men like Cortez and Pizarro, and that had once conquered empires, would not meekly lie down and sacrifice both freedom and religion to an alien ideology.

The bloodshed and carnage that resulted were far away and of no real interest to us until the cry went out for volunteers to help the defenders of the faith. Even then we took little notice; we were more concerned with our own immediate problems and discussion on a foreign war was rather low down on our nightly debating agenda. But when lads from our own street slipped quietly away to take up arms for God and Spain we were shaken from our insularity. It now became our major talking point. We soon convinced ourselves that dark and evil forces were ravaging a fair land, and that when they had completed the destruction of Spain they would turn their attention to Mother Ireland. We also were Catholic, and was not the grand plan of the evil ones to destroy our holy church? We would have to draw up plans to defend ourselves. As true Catholics and brave Irishmen we should be prepared to lay down our lives for faith and country.

Having unanimously agreed that immediate preparations were necessary in case of invasion, Frank stepped forward to announce that he had appointed himself commander-in-chief. There were no objections to this act of self-aggrandizement because we were all aware of the militarism that ran in his blood-line. His father had been a corporal in the Great War, had seen action on the battlefields of Flanders and, no doubt about it, would be a valuable source of information on military strategy. Another factor which weighed heavily in Frank's favour was the similarity in the names of himself and the Spanish Generalissimo. The lack of the "o" did not implant any doubts that he would be any less brilliant than the Spaniard.

"The first thing," said the General, "is the oath of allegiance. Let's all go home and get our catechisms, they will do as well as the bible." I saw a slight problem arising here as one of our gang was a Protestant, but Frank was equal to the occasion when it was pointed out to him.

"We'll make him an honorary Catholic for the swearing in, then he can go back to his own religion," said he, settling the matter to everybody's satisfaction.

The homes we were to defend were part of a terrace of houses that huddled together like a group of drunks drawing support from each other. They were of L-shaped design, the kitchen window of each looking onto the back wall of its neighbour. The gardens, some lawned, some turned over to vegetable production, were separated by five-foot-high stone walls, and terminated at the base of the twenty-foot-high perimeter wall of the army barracks.

Trenches were our number one priority, according to Frank. We would need many well-prepared trenches to fortify all our gardens. Good trenches had been the undoing of the Germans, and trenches would halt the Reds. Armed with an assortment of spades, forks and shovels we descended upon the General's garden. Ruling out any possibility of an attack from the flank, it was the General's considered opinion that the assault when it came would be over the barrack wall, because no matter how barbaric the

Red hordes might be they would never come through his mother's front door without her permission and that was something she would never grant, more especially if they had muddy boots.

The trench, when completed, was wall-to-wall across the garden, about three feet deep and almost as wide. Standing on the rampart, one arm across his chest, a hand tucked inside his jacket and the other arm hidden behind his back, like a diminutive Napoleon the General congratulated us on our achievement and went on to suggest that it was our Christian duty to supply all the other residents of the street with similar defences. We would carry out the work free, gratis and for nothing; in fact we would inform nobody what we were about until we were done. It would be a grand surprise when they eventually learned of our consideration for their welfare. Under the General's expert guidance and with the sense of urgency he instilled in us we made rapid progress in our neighbourly endeavours. The farther we progressed the more enthusiastic he became. He no longer partook in the spadework but paraded up and down, egging us on and orating like a demagogue: there would be no one more disappointed than he if an attack did not materialise. Such was his zeal, I began to have misgivings about accepting his leadership and feared that he might even be tempted to start his own war.

Deeply engrossed in our work we were nearly startled out of our wits by an ear-shattering roar. Peeping over the top of the trench we discovered that it had emanated from the owner of the lawn we were excavating. Having always considered him to be a real Irish gentleman, one of the old stock, we were completely taken aback by his sudden change of character as he came charging down the path bellowing like an enraged bull. He looked as if Satan had taken possession of his very soul. Of one thing we were certain – to stand and explain would be fatal. There was only one course open to us and, as one, we made for the nearest wall, blind panic taking hold. With the General in the lead by about fifty yards we put as many walls and gardens as we could between us and the raving maniac. There was no stopping until we reached our hideout, where we could feel sure we would be safe from what had appeared to be certain death.

Ashen-faced, trembling with shock, we gasped for breath before the questions came tumbling out. What had come over the man? Had he taken leave of his senses? Did his family have a history of insanity? Was there a full moon? What had we done to warrant such an outburst? We were only providing him with the defences he would surely need when the Reds arrived, and for free! If this was the attitude people were going to adopt we would do no more favours for anybody. What would he have said if we had left his the only undefended house in the street? He would not have liked it one bit. It would just serve him right if his were the only property to suffer when the war began.

Empty bellies are a marvellous antidote for fear, and it was the need for sustenance that instilled in us the courage to return to our homes. On rounding the corner of the street we were rooted to the pavement by the sight that met our eyes. All the women in the neighbourhood were stood around in earnest conversation, and there in their midst, gesticulating wildly, was the nut-case. The music had to be faced: as we tentatively approached, my mother grabbed me by the ear and quickly dragged me indoors. I was thankful to be delivered from the hands of that devil incarnate who was in a state of near apoplexy as he continued to rant and rave about his precious lawn. My mother was a most reasonable woman and always made it a point to ask questions first before belting me, which seemed to me to be a more acceptable practice than punishment before trial as was my father's wont. I tried to explain how we were endeavouring to protect our homes from the Red menace, but the logic of my argument was lost on her and in no way protected me from her wrath. I was then despatched to bed to await the further punishment I was certain to receive when my father arrived home. I lay in bed, enviously watching the flies enjoying life as they gave each other piggy-back rides around the bedroom ceiling, and pondered on the injustice of it all. I marvelled at the stupidity of adults, and wondered how they could be so oblivious to the danger we were all in.

I heard my father arrive home and the first words to issue from his mouth filled me with dread.

"Where is he?"

There was no need for my mother to fill him in on my day's adventures; some kindly, informative Christian had got to him and enlightened him with the lurid details. I was for it, and I got it, and for good measure was told that if all the gardens were not restored to their original state first thing in the morning there would be more of the same waiting for me tomorrow night.

We were herded together next morning under the watchful eyes of our mothers and ordered to fill in all our trenches, starting with Crazy Horse's, a name the demon was to carry for ever more. Somehow we did not find it as enjoyable a task as the excavations, and could find no heart for it. We all smarted from strap or switch and showed little inclination for work. Like helots we laboured with our shovels, our spirits at their lowest ebb. We were wrapped in a cloud of deep depression when fate took a hand to put the smiles back on our faces. We had an "air raid". It was not the kind of air raid we had been expecting and for which we had worked so hard to prepare. This raider was no Red; he was white. It was a seagull on a reconnaissance flight from the coast and as he zoomed overhead he took a notion to evacuate his bowels. His aim was faultless: with a sound like the crack of a whip he scored a direct hit on the ex-General's forehead. It was the final humiliation for Frank. He threw his shovel to the ground and stalked off in a rage as we rolled on the damp brown soil in paroxysms of laughter, the pains of the flesh, the injustice of adults, and the troubles of the world banished from our minds.

The Captain's Cap

S OME OF OUR greatest pleasures were those we derived from our local river: we spent all free, sunny moments there. What had in early spring been verdant banks would by late summer be threadbare trails to favoured pools where we dipped and splashed in a dalliance of delight. Without benefit of municipal swimming pools it was to these watering holes that we thronged during the long, hazy days of summer. Not even the occasional bloated and decaying carcass of a dog or sheep could dampen our enthusiasm for the cooling water, and by some divine fluke we were never infected with disease or pestilence.

We entered another world when we embarked on one of our expeditions. It would no longer be "our" river; it would be the Amazon, Nile or Congo. It was what we chose it to be. It became the habitat of crocodiles, octopuses, giant squid and piranah fish. It acquired bottomless depths, quicksands, whirlpools and other deadly perils. Fearless explorers all, we scorned such dangers as we struggled doggedly upstream bringing civilization to hitherto unknown tribes of headhunters dwelling along the riverbanks. With our shoes tied together and slung about our necks, we waded knee-deep in search of high adventure. How much more exciting our explorations would be if only we possessed a boat. Something in which we could skim over the water at a fast bat instead of risking life and limb painfully plodding barefoot through the rough stones and pebbles that littered the river-bed. It was a deprivation in need of remedy. Purchase was out of the question: between us we could not raise enough money in a year to buy an oar, never mind a boat. The most primitive tribes on earth owned boats, boats they had made themselves. If they could do it, why not we?

With our vastly superior technology there would be no reason to confine ourselves to an up-river craft; we could build one big enough and sturdy enough to take us down to the tidal reaches and all the way to the sea. It need not even end there. We could move out into the bay, cross over to Fenit or Camp, and never again have to wait for our parents to scrape up the train fares for·the annual excursions to those exotic resorts. We could row or sail over the waves at will and save all that expense. All that was required to turn dreams to reality was a tree and a few axes. Neither of these essentials posed a problem; nearly every home could boast an axe and Ballyseedy wood contained more than enough trees.

The first day of the summer holidays saw us marching up the river-bank, heading for the darkest section of the wood with an ample supply of jam sandwiches and armed to the teeth with our finely honed axes. We had agreed on the "dark" wood for our new enterprise not only for its abundance of trees but because here we would be free from the jealous eyes of rival gangs and safe from the restraints of interfering adults. Scouting around among the sturdy residents in search of a likely victim for felling we came upon a large chestnut that had reached the end of its days. It now lay supine, staring blindly towards the blue sky through the gap in the canopy it had once occupied. We sat upon the lifeless trunk, legs dangling, fished our dry butt-ends from their hiding places behind the lining of our jackets and lit up. What had for weeks filled us with enthusiasm now looked a daunting prospect. Faint hearts would have baulked, but we were hearties, Jasons to a man.

The morning was wasted by four brains chugging along four different tracks meandering nowhere. Frustrated by our inability to agree on whose axe should take the first chip from the trunk we arrived at the conclusion that one of us should shoulder full responsibility for the running of the show. The honour fell to Michael. It was not because he was the oldest of the gang, or the biggest, nor even because he was the best fist-fighter among us, but because he was experienced with boats. He had spent a holiday out in Dingle the previous summer with some cousins of his and had seen many curraghs and, what's more, had actually sat into some that had been brought ashore for repair. These were first-class qualifications that deserved loyalty and respect from us all. These we promised to give. Listening attentively to his acceptance speech we were convinced that we had made a wise decision and raised no objections when he asked that henceforth he should be addressed as "Captain".

"Right," said the Captain, "our first job is to build a boathouse."

The first rumblings of mutiny were heard over this decision: we had come here to build a boat, not a house.

"No good boat is without a boathouse," said the Captain in the manner of a man of wisdom and authority, "and besides, if we build it properly we can work in all weathers."

We had no answer to that, so we set to collecting materials and started construction on a site that the Captain had selected down by the waterside. By evening we had what he considered was a worthy home for our future craft.

It took the whole of the second day to hack off the required length from the massive trunk and to trim off the weighty superfluous branches. We now ran up against another unanticipated problem: how were we to get our stump to the boathouse? Try as we would, to roll or drag it the short distance proved to be beyond our combined capabilities. There was only one answer: reluctant though we were, we would have to resort to the recruitment of casual labour, blowing the gaff on our secret project. Every man has his price: bribery was our inducement. With a promise of a free trip across the bay we acquired several willing helpers. By the sweat of our brows, and more beside, we did labour. Hours of heaving and hauling, blood, sweat and curses finally saw the great baulk of timber under cover: the hard graft was over and from now on it was all downhill, or so we figured. Dismissing our casuals we paid them off with complimentary tickets. Empty cigarette packets were torn open and had inscribed on the back the handwritten promise, "valid for one return trip to Fenit", and duly signed by the Captain.

Throughout the early weeks of the holidays we beavered away at our task whatever the weather. Our shelter proved to be less impervious to rain than we had expected and there was more than one occasion after a heavy downpour when we would work in the nude, as our sodden clothes hung from surrounding branches drying in the breeze. As the days passed and the boat took shape we became more dedicated to the task. The Captain fuelled our enthusiasm as he expounded his dreams. He no longer saw it as a pleasure craft but as a money-making venture – a ferry boat. To facilitate the carrying of passengers two of the crew would have to stand down, which of course was unfortunate but unavoidable; as Captain he would sail on all voyages.

It was a day for celebration, flag waving, the rolling of drums and the blowing of trumpets, but there were none of these things. We just flopped down quietly to gaze in wonder at the miracle of our creative skills. It was ready for launching, the end product of all that sweat and toil.

"There is only one thing missing," said the Captain, disturbing the silence.

"What is that?" I enquired. "It looks all right to me."

"I haven't got a cap for the launch tomorrow," said Michael.

"What the hell do you want a bloody cap for?" asked Gerald rather sharply.

"Who ever heard of a Captain without a cap?" snapped Michael. "It's just not right."

"He's got a point there," piped up Frank, "how would anybody know he was the Captain if he's not wearing a proper cap?"

"Let him hang a sign around his neck," said Gerald, obviously annoyed that we should even be discussing such a triviality.

It was Frank who came to the rescue and helped save the situation from getting out of hand. His father, being a postman, had some old caps lying about the house; one of these could easily be transformed into a Captain's cap with the addition of a piece of white cloth and he would attend to that tonight.

We met on the bridge that fateful morning and true to his word Frank had brought the cap. Momentarily Michael was overcome with emotion; a lump came to his throat and a little moistness showed in his eyes as he tried to express his gratitude. The pillow-case that Frank's mother would never miss lent it a grand appearance. It wasn't a perfect fit, but Michael's ears did a sterling job in preventing it from falling over his eyes. He looked every inch the Captain as, shoulders back and arms swinging, he led the way up the river-bank to the wood.

We had already constructed a makeshift slipway from the boathouse so we had little difficulty manoeuvering the craft down to the water. It floated right way up at least, but, to our mutual disappointment, listed heavily to the side.

"Just a little trimming off one side," said Michael, hopefully but wrongly.

It took a lot of axe work and hard slogging, waist-deep in water. The more we trimmed one side the more it listed to the opposite as if in defiance, silently mocking our nautical ambitions. I began to doubt we would have anything left but, finally, we had her floating on an even keel. For the first time since the project began we would not have to walk home. We would row triumphantly down to the bridge, there to tie up overnight in readiness for her maiden voyage into tidal waters on the morrow.

It was time to board. The Captain insisted it was his prerogative to be first so we pulled her close to the bank and held her fast as he, in his brand new Captain's cap, stepped aboard. She rocked slightly as he lowered himself gently into position. We cast her adrift, with Michael grimly holding the sides, a look of apprehension on his face as she slowly developed another ominous list and water began lapping over the lower side.

It was then that the Captain made a decision ill-befitting the title and honour we had bestowed upon him. Instead of behaving in the time-honoured tradition of men of his rank he abandoned his ship. She rolled over as he scurried over the side, revealing himself to be no better than a dirty rat. He vanished into the depths, then bobbed to the surface, spitting water, gasping for breath and screaming for help. We turned our backs and dejectedly walked away from the craven coward who refused to go down with his ship, as the beautiful Captain's cap disappeared around the bend, taking our dreams of adventure on the high seas with it.

28

The Trail of '38

"I READ A SMASHING book last week, 'twas all about the goldminers up in the Klondike."

We were sitting on the low wall outside Gerald's house, whiling away a pleasant half-hour before tea, and Frank, who was a bit of a bookworm, was enlightening us on his latest acquisition from the Carnegie library.

"They just dug great big nuggets of gold out of the river and became millionaires overnight; at least, some of them did," he continued.

"California and Australia made rich men out of many too," said Gerald. "Gold was just lying around in the rivers waiting to be picked up. It's all gone now. We were born at the wrong time," he added regretfully.

"Wouldn't it be great if we could find some gold in our river?" I asked.

"Any fool knows there's no gold there," replied Gerald, "but I'll tell you what, there used to be diamonds up Foley's glen."

"Diamonds in Foley's glen? Don't talk daft man, I've been up there and I can tell you there's nothing but great big boulders," interjected Frank.

Gerald was not to be put down so easily.

"If you went to the Klondike today that's all you would find, but we all know that there was gold there once."

"There could still be some there today that the miners overlooked," said Frank.

"If that's the case, couldn't there still be diamonds in Foley's glen?" I asked.

"That's doubtful," replied Gerald, "though there might be no harm in looking."

"If it's fine we could go up there on Saturday," said Frank. "We can take some sandwiches and have a day out anyway."

I had never been to Foley's glen, though I had heard many tales about it and could even see it from where we were sitting. It was clearly visible as a dark scar on the side of the mountain, where some ancient giant was reputed to have hurled his axe. It was also said to contain the grave of Queen Scotia, buried where she fell when her steed failed in an attempt to leap the void. I was looking forward to the prospect of a visit in eager anticipation, diamonds or no diamonds.

Saturday dawned cloudless; perfect weather for our expedition into the wilderness in search of riches. Our route to the diggings took us past the suburban homes of the town's wealthy merchants, hiding behind high walls and tall trees, safely tucked away from the prying and envious eyes of the masses. Beyond these opulent abodes the road degenerated into a rough, uneven, dusty lane that became extremely hard on the feet. We passed the occasional thatched farmhouse with its large yard, humming manure heap and threatening dog, and the lonely, slated or corrugated-iron covered cottages of the humble farm-workers. I was ready to throw in the towel by the time we reached the foot of the mountain and would have turned back were it not for fear of facing the farm dogs on my own. With heads craned forward for signs of danger and reluctant feet pushing us on, we slowly forged ahead up the ever steepening track. As we climbed we came upon two more farmhouses where the only signs of life were a donkey gazing questioningly over a hedge, a few hens kicking up a dust-storm in one of the yards as they scratched avidly for titbits, the usual barking dog, and a lonely cow contentedly chewing on its cud.

As we rounded the next bend we were assailed by a flock of crazed geese that suddenly appeared out of nowhere. Charging, wings outstretched, necks craned and bills agape, they spat and hissed their goosey profanities at us. Our weary legs were spurred into new life as they carried our tired and aching bodies at high speed beyond the reach of those feathered maniacs. This sudden spurt quickly brought us out on the open mountain: a sea of purple heather undulating in the warm breeze, with here and there a hump-backed gorse bush, deformed at birth in its battle to survive in the almost constant south-westerly blows. Climbing onto a nearby bank we were rewarded with a close-up view of our El Dorado a couple of hundred feet below us. It was impossible to see the river itself through the density of the trees that huddled together as they sheltered in the narrow confines of the glen.

A sheep-track led us down to this oasis in a purple desert. The contrast to our own river was startling; there were no bottomless buckets here, no discarded car doors and mudguards and no rusting bicycle frames. The water looked like sparkling lemonade as it bubbled, splashed and danced its wild jig over the shining rocks to its own musical accompaniment. But we were in no mood to stand and stare or to revel in the beauty that surrounded us. Lust for diamonds and riches had brought us here and we were going to have them even if we had to tear the place apart.

Novices in the prospecting game, we had no idea how or where to start. If it were gold that we were seeking there would be no problem, we would have brought our frying pans and panned the fine gravel that littered the beds of the many pools, but diamonds were a different kettle of fish. How did they dispose themselves? Were they entombed in the boulders? Buried deep in the banks? Or were they simply to be found hiding in the nooks and crannies beneath the water? Lacking the foresight to bring tools we had to opt for the pools and put our trust in God.

It was every man for himself, staking out his claim to his own pool. Bending low, with my eyes close to the surface of the cool, clear water, I scanned the bottom for the glint of a sparkle that would betray pay-dirt. Nothing: nothing but multi-hued pebbles that had been worn round and smooth by a million years of fast-flowing water. Our predecessors had been thorough; they had stripped the place to the bone. Frank had been right: all this place contained was boulders and stones. I rose to straighten my aching back when Gerald suddenly leapt in the air, waving his arms above his head, shouting that he had found one. It was hard to tell which of us was more excited, Gerald at finding a diamond or Frank and I at the prospect of actually seeing one. Sitting on the grassy bank, he held out his hand and there, slightly bigger than a marble, was a rough, semi-transparent stone with a slight tinge of purple running through it.

"That's not a bloody diamond, it's not sparkling," said Frank.

"Of course it is, it's just got to be cut and polished, you fool," Gerald cut in. "Just goes to show what you know about diamonds."

"All right then smart arse, how much is it worth?" Frank was piqued.

"At a rough guess I'd say a hundred pounds; yes, a hundred pounds."

Gerald didn't sound too sure of himself, but we were prepared to take his word for it. At least he knew what a raw diamond looked like, which was more than could be said for Frank and myself.

"He's rich, Gerald is rich," I thought as we turned and ran to our respective pools to resume our frantic search.

Gerald made another strike, quickly followed by Frank,

Key ideas...

- Love as the motive force behind everything.
- Love also the ultimate cause of hostility which springs up when love is hindered.
- The three causes of duality and hostility:
  - Limiting love to a small circle;
  - The idea of other;
  - The desire to control.
- The unity of love and knowledge – love unites, knowledge illuminates.

Practices for the week...
(to be read every morning)

- Do not keep love within a small circle. Let it expand according to the need of the moment.
- Do not treat anyone as other than oneself.
- Do not seek to control those whom we love. Love always gives freedom from control.
- Let love and knowledge work together, with knowledge supporting and expanding love and love strengthening and completing knowledge.
- Continue to practise the Exercise.

Quotations...

- Love is the motive force behind all the processes at work in the world to sustain it. It could never be sustained without love. In the case of human life, its examples are the love of parents, the love of brothers, the love of friends and colleagues, etc. Even the behaviour of insects and moths seem to be based on some form of love. So much so, that the ultimate cause of hostility is also love, because hostility springs up when love is hindered. Thus a duality of love and hostility prevails everywhere. We want a thing we love; if we do not get it, we turn hostile. A love free from the above duality is true love.

  (Shri Shantananda Saraswati, 'Good Company', p.35)

◢ Love and knowledge are the same thing but the function of love is to join together and that of knowledge to tell, to illuminate.

In love, knowledge is helpful. For strengthening knowledge, love is essential. In the absence of love, knowledge would not be powerful enough to influence people. Knowledge only helps us to decide what is right and wrong, but it cannot alter things; love can alter them.

Without love, knowledge is incomplete and without knowledge love is incomplete because, in the absence of knowledge, love would go away. If there is knowledge, then love would be maintained. As love increases, knowledge also goes on increasing. Without knowledge, love is not expansive; and without love, knowledge is not allowed to play its full part.

(Shri Shantananda Saraswati, 'Good Company', p.148)

PRACTICAL
PHILOSOPHY
THE LOVE AND APPLICATION OF WISDOM
Sept. 2013

whose stone, though only slightly smaller than Gerald's first, was valued by him as being worth only fifty pounds. He said he could detect a slight flaw in it, but enough to lower its value. Accepting Gerald as our assayer we took his assessment without question and resumed our search. Try as I might, good fortune evaded me as the other two made more frequent strikes. It was time I had a word with Himself.

"Please, God, let me find just a little diamond and I promise not to look at the *Dandy* at Mass again."

The powers of prayer were proven to me beyond all doubt as I immediately uncovered my first find. The bad spell had been broken and I was now picking up gems as quickly as the other two. Moving upstream from pool to wealth-laden pool, each one releasing even more treasure, we were becoming wealthy beyond our wildest dreams. Taking a break for a smoke and to assess the situation we decided to call it a day when we had amassed a thousand pounds each; that would be enough to keep us in luxury for the rest of our lives, and there was no point in being too greedy. Though it crossed my mind I neglected to mention that our pockets would be hard put to contain that amount, not to mind any more.

As the sun departed the lonely glen so did we, trousers suspended six inches lower on braces stretched to their utmost limits with the weight of gems in the bulging pockets.

"How will we exchange all this for money?" enquired Frank.

"We will take them to the jewellers on Monday," replied Gerald. "Murphy will be glad to get his greedy hands on this little lot."

"Are you sure he's got that much money?" I asked, unable to accept that anybody could be so rich.

"If he hasn't we can go somewhere else," said Gerald, "but I can't see him letting these slip through his fingers."

"We better not let anybody else know about this," he continued as he staggered along before us, shoulders bowed under the weight and trousers bouncing up and down like a yo-yo. "We'll stop off at Desmond castle and hide the stuff till Monday," he proposed. "Nobody will find it there; we can keep an eye on it till dark."

We hid our cache under a pile of stones inside the castle wall, relieved to have the weight removed from our shoulders. We hung around outside the castle, taking it in turns to go home for some grub so as to keep constant guard on our hoard until dark. We were confident that it would be safe through the night because of the ghosts that were reputed to walk through the castle and its grounds between dusk and dawn. If the place were haunted at night it was also haunted throughout Sunday, we never leaving the place out of our sight for a moment.

On Monday morning when every kid on the street was heading for school, we were quietly transferring our hoard into the flour-sack Gerald had brought and hiding our satchels in the nook that had previously housed the diamonds. Over the weekend we had decided to pool our resources until after the deal was finalised, then split the dough three ways. With Gerald leading the way, and Frank and I trailing behind carrying the bag of precious stones between us, we took a circuitous route to town. We rested our load on the pavement outside Murphy's jewellery shop while Gerald rummaged around inside the bag to select what he described as a "good specimen". "Now let me do the talking," he said, as we picked up the bag to follow him in. "I'll get a good price on this one; then, when he's paid up, empty the sack on the counter. That'll shake him."

"Yes, what can I do for you gentlemen?" asked the smartly dressed man behind the counter, his nose twitching as if there was a bad pong in the air.

"This," said Gerald, oozing self-confidence. "How much

are you going to give us for this?"

"Nothing," said the gentleman without batting an eyelid.

"Nothing?" Gerald's blood was up. "Nothing for a good quality diamond? Have we got the wrong man? Fetch your diamond expert, someone who knows a good bargain when he sees it."

"Oh, there's no need for that attitude, I can see it's a diamond all right: a Kerry diamond. A quartz stone. Worthless. Good day to you, gentlemen."

"Oh, by the way," he called as we turned to leave the shop, "if you want some more, you can get tons of them up Foley's glen."

Fauntleroy

TO A FISHERMAN down there in the Gulf of Mexico the soft breeze fanning his brow would be a welcome relief from the heat of the day. To a few lads far away in Ireland that same breeze would be their passport to the pictures.

Like others of its kind, our young breeze would break from its confines and head out over the open sea to follow the traditional migratory trail to cooler climes. On its long journey, avidly scooping moisture from the crests of the waves, it would reach Ireland gorged beyond its capacity to contain. The stiff climb over the first high grounds would sap it of its remaining strength and compel it to offload its liquid cargo. The resultant precipitation might be spasmodic, light-heartedly accepted by the unfortunate recipients as showers. Perhaps the overflow might be more prolonged and produce what was laughingly termed "a soft day". There were times too when these waterlogged visitors from the south-west took a fancy to our locality and lingered to outstay their welcome, becoming wet blankets to all but those of us who were aware of the truth in the saying, "every cloud has a silver lining". The longer and heavier the rains fell the more likely they were to produce the pennies. From dingle and dell, through gutter and gully, the downward swirl led to our friendly river. Rising to the challenge, she would struggle to cope, but would be thwarted in her endeavours by the twice-daily tides. The volume of salt water rammed down her throat, acting as an emetic, would result in her retching over the surrounding countryside.

With the first break in the sky it was all hands to the bridge to survey the extent of the flood waters. The road dipped beyond the bridge and invariably suffered the same watery fate as the saturated fields, becoming a hindrance and irritant to motorists and cyclists alike but revenue to the gang. There was a set scale of fees for our services: sixpence to push a car through the murky waters and threepence to transport a bike to the other side as the owner made his or her precarious way along the low wall. For the daring motorist who, to save himself a "tanner", risked the fording and became immobilized, rescue would cost a shilling. The work continued until darkness fell, when late travellers were abandoned to their own salvation. Homeward bound, we were tired and light-hearted but heavy trousered; unfortunately, more often than not the weight of the trousers owed more to waterlogging than to cash in the pockets.

A part-time member of the gang, and one who dared not go home with his clothes wet and muddy, was one Little Lord Fauntleroy. He was dubbed with this moniker on the first day his family moved to the street because of his immaculate attire and his ability to remain neat and tidy in any circumstances. He repelled dirt and grime as easily as we attracted it: we were literally poles apart. His mother was a snob and deeply resented her little blue-eyed boy associating with the rabble, but there was little she could do about it short of confining him to the house all day. She was also a domineering virago who ruled the home with a rod of iron and it was more from fear than natural talents that Fauntleroy owed his sanitary sartorial demeanour.

A bad day comes everybody's road now and again: one of those days when everything seems to go wrong, when one feels that it would have been wiser to have stayed in bed.

Young Fauntleroy had not been long running with the pack when one of those misfortune-laden days came his way. It occurred during one of our high flood periods, when the rains had not let up for over three days and the depth of water on the road was above knee level. It was Fauntleroy's first experience of picking up a little pocket money on the side and he was enjoying it immensely. With shoes and socks neatly stowed in a hole in the wall and his trousers carefully rolled up to the tops of his thighs he was putting heart and soul into the job.

It was an exceptionally busy day, cars were lined up on both sides of the flood waiting to be moved safely across the murky, brown waters. Trade was good and all was going well until we came up against Smart Alec. His idea of a good joke would be stealing candy from a baby or kicking the crutch out from under a cripple. Seeing there was the chance of another cheap laugh he took advantage of it, and before we had pushed him clear of the water he switched on the engine, threw the car into gear and was away like a scalded cat, waving a hand through the window. Fauntleroy was taken by complete surprise and hurled headlong into the water. Floundering for a few moments like a beached whale before staggering to his feet, he took stock of his predicament and burst into tears.

He could never go home in this state; it would have been bad enough to have got his trouser bottoms wet but this was catastrophic. He would have to run away, join a tinker band, or perhaps Duffy's circus, but face his mother – never. Gerald, with his practical turn of mind, quickly came up with a solution to the problem. There would be no need for Fauntleroy to take to mending pots and pans, nor for that matter to taming lions and tigers. We would all go to Jamsie's, light a good fire in his outhouse and have those sodden clothes nice and dry before teatime.

Jamsie was one of the "characters" of which our town had more than its fair quota. A semi-recluse and extremely eccentric, dressing in the style that a quarter of a century later would come back into fashion amongst the "Teddy boys", he lived alone in the basement of a large three-storey house, the upper floors of which he sub-let to provide a small income for his frugal needs. An archway passed beneath one end of the house and led to a large yard in which stood the crumbling remains of old stables. Behind this outhouse was a small garden, residence of a gnarled old crab-apple tree which Jamsie proudly referred to as his "orchard", laying into us with his walking stick whenever he caught us scrumping.

A rickety wooden door was the only means of access to the old ruin. It had been designed to slide but had probably never moved along its track since long before Jamsie had bought his last suit of clothes. Prizing it out at the bottom and spragging it open, there was just enough room for us to pass through one at a time. The loft had long ago collapsed and despite the gaping holes in the roof there was plenty of dry fuel lying about the rough, uneven floor. We soon had a good blaze going and huddled around to warm our hands as Fauntleroy, teeth chattering audibly, dripped copiously, creating a pool about his feet that threatened to spread and extinguish our source of comfort.

"You'll never dry out like this," said Gerald, taking control of the exercise. "Get them off, they'll have to be wrung out. If we all hold them to the fire they'll soon dry."

Standing there in his birthday-suit, as close as he dared to the crackling fire, Fauntleroy tried to get a little heat into his blue, goose-pimpled flesh. Each of us holding an item of his gear, we laughed and joked as we watched the steam mingle with the smoke that drifted up and through the openings in the roof. The cruel jokes that gave us so much hilarity were entirely directed at our naked and woebegone comrade, belying any expressions of sympathy we tossed in his direction.

Our ribald laughter came to an abrupt end when we

saw Jamsie forcing his way through the gap in the doorway, his dreaded walking stick in his hand, the fires of
Hades in his eyes and the wrath of God written on his
angry face. The grip we had on Fauntleroy's clothes was
relinquished, to be replaced by the grip of fear in our
hearts as he came at us, his stick whistling through the
air in an endeavour to flail us alive. We fled in all directions to avoid its cutting bites, all of us that is except
Fauntleroy who was fighting valiantly to save his clothes
from being engulfed in flames. He was a sitting duck for
Jamsie. We could hear the crack of wood on bare flesh
through Fauntleroy's screams and Jamsie's curses as like
demented maniacs we tore the door from its moorings in
our frantic bid to escape. When he had eventually to
decide whether to save his clothes from the flames or his
miserable hide from further punishment, Fauntleroy
opted for the latter. Abandoning his still soaking togs to a
fiery end he charged through the doorway, overtaking us
as we fled through the archway. He tore out onto the
street like a bat out of hell and made a bee-line for home.

Lady Luck had already deserted him twice in one day
and was about to do the dirt on him for the third time.
Having done a record-shattering streak down the street he
turned in through his front gate, only to be confronted by
his mother, whom the gods decreed should choose that
precise moment to go to the shop. What passed through
the woman's mind as she came face to face with her stark-
naked son has never been recorded, but the memory of the
screams that emanated from the front bedroom as shaving
strop made contact with already sore flesh is deeply
imbedded in my mind.

Only a Dog

I WAS SORRY to see the Murphys leave: they had been good neighbours and many's the penny the old lady had given me for running for her messages. It wasn't just the money I would miss, it was their attitude that had most impressed me. Though they had passed the three score and ten milestone on their journey to the Celestial City they always had a kind word for those of us who were just setting out, never forgetting that they too had once trod on the same stretch of trail. The only enemy they ever had was that nasty old man with the scythe and he was now running hard on their heels. What time they had left before he finally caught up with them they had decided should be spent with their daughter, and so they had upped and moved to Dublin. It was in one of that city's "dailies" from which my mother was to read aloud to me less than a year later the brief announcement: "Murphy, at her residence...". A few lines in a newspaper had brought to a close another chapter in the book of life.

Within a few days of the Murphys vacating the house another elderly couple had moved in; a couple who, like the Murphys, I would always remember, but, unlike their predecessors, not for who or what they were but for what they had brought with them – a black and white middle-aged scruff of a fox terrier.

I was no stranger to the domesticated animal. Belonging to a family of cat worshippers I had learned to

41

accept unquestioningly subjugation under the domineering paw of the feline, but my knowledge of the canine was rudimentary and amounted to little more than the occasional tail-wagging salutation from a passing mutt. I had often questioned my mother about the prospect of acquiring a dog but was always fobbed off with an, "I've got enough mouths to feed as it is".

It could have been the bone, or maybe it was the few kind words I threw to her that decided Rose, our new quadruped neighbour, to sniff me out for her single-minded attention. Whatever it was, she saw in me deliverance from the monotony and dull routine of life with her elderly owners the Flynns. She had figured out for herself that there should be more to a dog's life than confinement to house and garden, with the odd stroll on the end of a leash. As if she had mastered the art of telepathy her soulful pleading eyes and plaintive whimperings nagged at my conscience, haunting me until I developed a guilt complex and loaded onto my young shoulders the blame for her incarceration. Before I cracked up I had to have it out with her, I had to encourage her to find another mug.

"Why don't you get off my back Rose? Will you please leave me alone?"

She opened her mouth, her tongue flopped out and she laughed at me, her stump of a tail grabbing her rear end and shaking it vigorously. I was beaten.

"Oh, all right then," I said as I brushed past her and knocked on the door. "Is it all right for me to take Rose for a walk Mister Flynn?" I asked timidly.

"Of course it is lad, but be careful she doesn't get run over," he replied easily.

A lack of vocal chords was no impediment to Rose and, as if understanding what was being said she turned to leave, looked over her shoulder and growled at me to get a move on, as though she were afraid her owner would change his mind.

I did not take her very far on our first outing. I had shouldered a responsibility for which I had not prepared myself. Mister Flynn's parting words had worried me. Caring less for any pain or suffering that she might endure, and more for what might happen to my own miserable hide if she met with an accident, I took her no farther than the end of the street. Unconcerned about my misgivings she contented herself with investigating the odours and aromas of canine appeal. Like a bloodhound hot on the trail of a felon she scouted along before me, her nose vacuuming the pavement, raising no objections when I called her to heel and sniffing her way home with the same zeal as when we had started out.

For a few days I buried my head in the sand trying to kid myself that what I didn't see did not exist, but to no avail; I had started something so I was obliged to continue it. The whimpering and plangent lamentations I fiercely resisted, but the offer of a few pennies from old man Flynn caught me in a weak spot. He saw in me an escape from what he considered a chore – taking Rose for a twice-daily constitutional. Every walk out took us farther afield and became of longer duration until we came to spending the whole of my free time together. She became an honorary gang member, joining in our games and in our river and woodland adventures. She took to the water as if it were her natural environment, displaying an aquatic versatility that would shame an otter. To say that her breast- and backstroke were comparable with her dog-paddle might be a slight exaggeration, but that she was the best swimmer that ever dipped a paw nobody could deny.

The wood was a treasure-house filled with a wealth of sound and scent; a web of tracks and trails that tantalized and teased with the promise of game. Her ears pricked and nose twitched in response to every sound or smell that wafted on the soft breezes that filtered through the undergrowth, winding her like a watch-spring before she uncoiled to spurt off on some fruitless chase. Saliva dripping from a steaming tongue, she would return to flop in the cooling grass and cast me an eye that seemed to say, "I nearly got him that time".

In the beginning she went straight home when we returned from our expeditions, had her dinner and later called around to say goodnight before waddling off to bed. But as time went on she became reluctant to spend any but eating time with her own folk. She hung around our door even after I had been packed off to bed and stayed there until called in by the Flynns when they were about to retire. Flynn felt that he was losing the affections of his dog and forbade me to have any more to do with her. He said he felt it was in her best interest if I did not even speak to her. He ensured that she would not call around for me by tethering her to a stake in the garden and hoped that in time she would see the folly of her disloyal behaviour.

His efforts were in vain: she had decided where her future lay and every time she got the opportunity she was off, making a bee-line for our house. He had lost her loyalty and eventually realised the fact. His final solution was drastic and, to me, petty and small-minded. He knew that he had lost her but did not possess the magnanimity to grant her desire; instead, in a fit of pique, he banished her to a life of penal servitude on his brother's farm about twenty miles from town.

For several days I was steeped in gloom and depression; I felt that if he had held any affection for her at all he could at least have transferred her to my care. My mother, despite her earlier protests about the expense of keeping a dog, liked Rose and would have welcomed her into the family. She did promise that if it would make things any easier for me she would look out for a pup and would give it a home if I promised to look after it, but I wasn't to be consoled and rejected the offer. If I could not have Rose I wanted no other dog, no substitute could ever be acceptable. But my dejection was short-lived, my feelings were fickle and my loss was soon to be dissolved and dissipated in the frivolous pursuit of childish pleasures. Within a few weeks of her departure I had forgotten her.

One year later, almost to the day, I was enjoying my Saturday lie-in when my mother entered the bedroom to announce that I had a visitor.

"Who's looking for me at this hour of the morning?" I asked rather crankily.

"You'd better get up and come and see," she replied, laughing.

My visitor was impatient. I heard a door crash open, the patter of racing feet, and into the room and onto the bed charged Rose. Her joy and rapture was overwhelming, from nose to tip of tail her body vibrated in ecstacy, her tongue lashed my face covering me in saliva as she whimpered excitedly: "I've come home, I've come home". I laughed, squeezing her tightly as she fussed and fawned. I saw a moistness in my mother's eyes as she turned quietly to leave the room, then realisation hit me and I burst into tears.

For the first time in my life I saw myself as I really was: selfish, shallow and egotistic. How long had I remembered Rose? What depth had my affection been? What did I know of love? Love was only a word to express an emotion that nobody could know the true meaning of until it was experienced. Yet here was a dumb animal that did know, that had not forgotten, that had remembered during every minute of every day and that had traversed twenty miles of unknown country to fulfill that love. She had demonstrated the true meaning of man's most lightly used four-letter word.

"We'll have to tell Mister Flynn," said my mother when we joined her in the kitchen.

"Why? She's not his dog; he gave her away."

"That's why, she belongs to his brother."

"Who's going to tell him?" I queried.

"You are," she said. "Get out there straight away and get it over with."

"Rose is in our house, Mister Flynn. She came back last night," I said nervously when he opened the door.

"Well, well, I'll be. After all this time?" was his comment.

"Do you want her back Mister Flynn?" I asked apprehensively.

"I don't want her, she's my brother's dog now. We'll have to see what he says."

"How long will that be?"

"Not till the next time he comes to town. You'll have to look after her till then; that is, if you don't mind."

"Oh, I don't mind at all," I answered as I rushed away to tell my mother.

It was two weeks before the farmer called to see his brother, and it was two weeks of living hell. I dreaded every day, fearing that each would be the last of our resumed association. She came to the front gate to see me off to school every morning and according to my mother she moped around until some internal clock told her it was time for my return, when she again took up her position at the gate to welcome me home. At school I was the one to do the moping, neglecting my education and laying myself open to the strap for lack of attention and concentration. Dread stalked me home until I turned the corner to see her patiently waiting.

Her owner came and went without my seeing him. He had given her up for dead, and when he had learned of her whereabouts and the reason for her long journey he told his brother that I could keep her. She had never been of any use to him anyway, always wandering off if she weren't chained up. He had wanted a ratter and she had turned out to be a dosser. Besides, he had replaced her with a far better dog.

It was only another week to the long summer holidays and luckily for Rose a period in my life when I was entering the exploration stage, wanting to see if the grass was really greener over the hill and curious to know if those faraway cows did have longer horns. The gang had long been planning far-ranging expeditions and our first objective was the home-town of the Wild Colonial Boy. I knew that a lass experienced in long-distance walking would jump at the invitation to accompany us.

For lads who revelled in adventure like Michael, Frank, Gerald and myself, a jaunt over a little mountain like Slieve Mish didn't seem too daunting a prospect. Sol, the sun, was still rubbing the sleep from his eyes when Rose and I slipped out of the house without telling anyone of our plans and joined the others to set off on the long trek. We passed Foley's diamond-laden glen without as much as a glance and headed for the summit that basked in the sun beckoning us. We were suckered; what we had believed to be the summit turned out to be the top of a rise giving way to a large dip that sloped up in the distance to what surely must be the real summit. We were conned again and again; it was like trudging up and down a giant never-ending switch-back. We would have jacked it in and turned back were it not for the thought that for the rest of our lives we would be haunted with the question, "was the rise we had turned our back on the one we had been seeking?" The only one that didn't grumble and complain was Rose, and Rose was the only one that didn't gasp in awe when we topped the final rise to see the panorama that was spread out before us.

In greens, yellows and browns the fields of the valley of the Maine were spread out like a giant multi-coloured carpet, disappearing into the east under cover of a heat haze. To the south and stretching out to the west was the blue and purple grandeur of the Reeks and the craggy mountains of Iveragh, while below and to our right Dingle Bay lay peacefully lazing the day away. After a short rest we descended to the little village where Jack Duggan had spent his boyhood, quenched our thirsts with lemonade and ice-cream and mooched around gawping open-mouthed as if we were tourists. We wandered down by the river, where I had to keep a tight rein on Rose. The tide was on the ebb and the fast-flowing water looked too menacing for my liking. Though the sun shone brightly the water and banks glowered dark and threatening and prompted me to suggest we return home.

Reaching the foot of the mountain we baulked at the prospect of the long, arduous, uphill slog and voted instead to take the long way around on the main road in the hope that we might be able to cadge a lift. Rose proved to be a liability in this endeavour. Many cars stopped to offer assistance but none were prepared to take on board a scruffy terrier. It had grown dark by the time we rounded the end of the mountain and saw the lights of town twinkling like stars in the dim distance; warm, welcoming beacons to five foot-sore travellers.

There was no band, there was no bunting and there were no flags, but there were lots of people. Cheers went up and backs were slapped as we pushed our way through the crowds like conquering heroes returning from the wars.

"What's going on?" we asked.

"We all thought ye were dead," came the reply. "Search parties have been out looking for ye, ye've never been seen all day."

We had dropped a clanger. None of us had told anyone where we were going and we had been away over sixteen hours; no wonder there was anxiety. We were in the soup now all right and I expected my hide to be as sore as my feet before I got to bed. To my surprise, things turned out differently. I was welcomed home with open arms such was the relief to discover I was not lying at the bottom of the river, though I was severely admonished for not leaving word as to where I was spending the day.

This had been the first of Rose's long-distance adventures at my side; she was to go north and climb the Stacks mountains, east through the woods, lanes and fields of the hinterland and west to the coast. Her journeys to the sea were her most pleasurable, satisfying her delight and fascination with water. Not satisfied with her long swim along the canal she would spend her day bobbing in the waves that rose and crashed on the shingle- and stone-covered shore. If our return journey from the coast coincided with the approach of the little train on its return from Dingle she took great pleasure from worrying the guard as he ran along beside the track trying to dislodge us from a bogie-bolster on which we would hitch a lift.

For three years her days were full and her life was good, and except for school hours she hardly left my side; she was my constant companion, where there was one there was the other. We were in total rapport, bound together in spiritual union like two halves of a single entity. Ever lively and bubbling with energy, it never crossed my mind that she was growing old until the day I noticed that her eyes were losing their sparkle. At first I thought it was a trick of the light, but when it showed up in the best of light I drew my mother's attention to it.

"I'm afraid she is going blind," said she gently.

"Isn't there something we can do for her?" I pleaded.

"I'm afraid not. She's got cataracts; it's going to get worse."

It did. Slowly and insidiously the milky-white veil spread and thickened over her dark brown eyes, creating a world of shadows.

"You should drown her," said Flynn, "there's no point in keeping a blind dog."

"Nobody's going to drown her, she's not blind," I

snapped at him.

"She soon will be. What'll you do then?"

"I'll look after her, she'll be all right," I told him.

The first indication that her blindness had become total was when she bumped into a chair that had been left in the middle of the kitchen floor. She had been without sight for some time but had been finding her way around by smell and familiarity with her surroundings. To help her with her handicap we had to ensure that in house and garden there had to be a place for everything and everything had to be kept in its place. She managed quite well with these arrangements and if it were not for the white film that clouded her eyes no one would have noticed that she was blind. Her internal clock was still working well and she continued to go to the front gate to await my return from school. She still enjoyed the odd dip in the river, but there were two irrevocable changes to her life style: she had to take her walks on the end of a lead and her rabbit-hunting days were over.

She was happy enough in her own way and I had become reconciled to caring for a blind dog, accepting it as one of the responsibilities of ownership, but I was unprepared for the suddenness with which the second blow fell. My mother took me aside when I came home to find that Rose was not at her post but lying quietly on her blanket.

"Rose is very ill and I don't think she has long more to live."

I was stunned, and for a few moments I couldn't bring myself to speak.

"I've not told you before," my mother continued, "but I have been noticing spots of blood where she lies. I've asked Mister Flynn to have a look at her and he said she has a growth in her stomach."

"What sort of growth?" I asked. "Can't it be cured?"

"I'm afraid not. Mister Flynn says it would be a kindness to put her out of her misery."

"I know what he wants to do, he wants to drown her," I cried, choking with tears.

Rose was lying on her bed, awake but making no attempt to come to me. I knelt beside her, lifted her head and cradled it in my arms. She looked up sightlessly and turned to lick my hand.

"You'll be all right Rose," I sobbed, "I'll not let Flynn touch you."

The unease followed me to school next day and tormented me through the early morning lessons. I could not get it out of my mind that Rose was in danger, that if I did not go home as soon as possible I would never see her again. I raised my hand to attract the teacher's attention, told him I was feeling ill and asked permission to leave. Burdened down with fears and apprehension I raced home with the fleetness of a greyhound, burst into the kitchen and saw at a glance that both Rose and her blanket were missing.

"Where is Rose?" I screamed at my mother.

"Mister Flynn has taken her for . . ."

I did not wait to hear her out. If Flynn had taken her I knew their destination. I turned and bolted in the direction of the river, blinded with tears and praying to God it was not too late. I stopped dead in my tracks: the invisible thread that had bound us together had been broken. I knew in my soul that there was no more need to hurry — Rose was dead.

Slowly I resumed my steps, isolated in my grief from the world around me. There were no more tears; my emotions were numbed, my senses dulled. I was unaware of Flynn's approach, I did not understand what he was saying, but his parting words echoed and re-echoed through my brain as I continued walking: "She was only a dog."

I flopped on the bank beside her final resting place — the water she had loved. I saw the sack anchored to the bottom, swaying in the current just beneath the surface. I had failed her: I had not been there when she had most needed me. I begged for her forgiveness, collapsing in a flood of tears. Haunting me as I sobbed myself into an exhausted sleep on that green and lonely bank were Flynn's parting words: "She was only a dog."

The Poacher

M Y LIFE-LONG FRIENDSHIP with Danny might never have been had it not been for my preoccupation with Mammon. Danny was a hick: he belonged on the other side of the tracks, or, to be more exact, the other side of the river. He was a lad of the sticks, and had nothing whatsoever in common with us streetwise urchins. It was not that we held anything against the hinterland and those who lived in it but, when all was said and done, they were our inferiors. The countryside was fine for a day out now and then, but who in his right mind would want to live in it?

Ours was a more modern, enlightened life style; our daily living did not end with the going down of the sun. We had our friendly street-lamp beneath which we could continue with our social activities until tiredness or parental command decreed otherwise. We were well aware as we frolicked and enjoyed our late evenings that those poor wretches were confined within their halfpenny-candle-illuminated hovels. The rung they occupied on humanity's evolutionary ladder was far beneath ours, though we were prepared to admit that they had progressed beyond the Neanderthal level of the mysterious tribes that dwelt beyond the mountains in the county of Cork.

It takes all kinds to make a world and it was no concern of ours how others choose to live, that was their own affair. All in all, relations between our two societies were amicable: they allowed us free access through their fields when bird-nesting, blackberry picking or mushrooming, and we, in our turn, allowed them unhindered passage through our street in their donkey-carts, even if it did disrupt our ball-games.

Our ideas of superiority over the country-boys were, on the whole, illusory, juvenile exercises in self-deception. They never appeared to be short of a bob or two while we were always scratching and scraping to supplement our Saturday penny. It was not that our parents were poor, because they were not, though some were less well-heeled than others. Our impecunious predicament was the end result of an attitude of mind and a parental sense of values. We had to learn the hard way the true value of money; it did not grow on trees and had to be worked for. There were few yokels who did not own a bicycle, or have easy access to one. Their journeys to town were usually accomplished on a saddle or the seat of a pony-trap while we made do by Shanks' pony, and that was a bitter pill to have to swallow.

Even more sour to the taste-buds was to see them smugly and laboriously pedal past with wheels almost buckling under the weight of furry corpses. It was the season for rabbits and we knew that now they were making real dough. There was brass in bunnies, and the countryside was overrun with them. There were more than enough to go around and catching rabbits would be far more lucrative than scratching in dustbins for jamjars. There was only one small problem: we knew nothing at all about trapping; the subject had no place on the school curriculum, so to further our education along these lines we would have to make discreet enquiries among the practitioners of the trade.

"Where are you taking all those bloody rabbits?" we politely enquired, as we stepped out in front of the bumpkin who looked least likely to offer resistance to four brave

54

townies.

"I'm taking them to the butcher's," he replied in a lazy drawl.

"What's the pay-off?" I asked in a fair imitation of one of the "Dead End Kids", hoping thus to further intimidate him.

"A bob or two apiece," he came back easily.

Here was this rather easy-going peasant, with about a dozen rabbits dangling from the handlebars of his fairly dilapidated bone-shaker, making a mint, while we had not enough between us to buy five fags.

"How can we get in on the act?" enquired Frank.

"Go out and snare them," came the curt reply.

We had to decide there and then whether to pocket our pride and reveal to this clodhopper our ignorance of even the most basic rudiments. Taking his cue from our nods of assent Frank spoke for all when he asked, "Will you show us how?"

"Of course I will. Sure, 'tis no bother. I'll see you on my way back," he answered as he jumped on his bike and ped-alled away towards town.

We did not have long to await his return. When he did arrive he introduced himself as Danny and invited us out to his ranch for our "get rich quick" instructions. He put the kettle on and treated us to some tea before disappear-ing to attend to some minor but necessary chores. When he returned he was armed with a handful of ready-made snares. Showing us how they operated by passing his hand through the loop of one he had set up we saw how quickly a rabbit could be trapped in the circle of death. The next stage was to make our own snares and under his expert guidance that was soon accomplished. Then came the most important lesson, how and where to set them. There was no point in staking them out anywhere in a field, they had to be set on the rabbit run, and not just anywhere on the run but at very specific points. We were good pupils, or maybe he was a good teacher; in any case he did not need the use of a leather strap to beat the lessons into us. We spent the evening with him and accompanied him out to the neighbouring fields to help him lay his own traps.

He had provided us with an ample supply of wire, which he trusted us to pay for out of our first profits, and as it was getting late we prepared to return home. Danny was staying out in the fields a little longer; he had to watch over his snares as poachers stalked the land like a plague, stealing both the snares and catches of honest men. If we were to take our new enterprise seriously then we would have to be equally vigilant; we would need to be on our guard last thing at night and first thing in the morning. He let us go with a graphic description of the fate that befell those who indulged in the despicable practice of poaching.

Late the following afternoon we checked our snares, prepared our pegs and headed out to the country. Outside town we decided to pair off, Gerald and Michael going in one direction and Frank and I in another. On Frank's suggestion we took the road towards Lamb's Rock: according to what he had heard rabbits were so numerous around this area they had to do their grazing on a shift basis. We laid out twelve traps, from which we confidently expected to achieve one hundred per cent success. We hung around until it was almost dark before we set off for home, confident that we would not be robbed of our catches, at least, not this side of dawn. Before parting company we agreed to meet at five o'clock next morning, though how either of us would be able to honour that commitment slightly puzzled me. When I informed my mother that I was having an early night she laid her hand on my brow under the impression that I was harbouring a fever, and when I announced that I intended to be up before five she blessed herself, bewildered by the sudden change that had come over me and fearing it could only be for the worse.

I found sleep elusive; dreams of wealth flooded my mind. I tried the traditional counting of sheep as an anti-dote for my insomnia but lost track of them as they disap-peared beneath a sea of rabbits. The more I twisted and turned the more our new entrepreneurial venture expand-ed, until by the time I eventually drifted into oblivion we were the country's most successful rabbit-meat moguls.

Sleep, when it did come, was fitful, shallow and brief. I slid from the bed, dressed and glided like a shadow to the kitchen, disturbing not a soul but the dog. I'll swear to my dying day she glanced at the clock before turning over to resume her slumber. It was a few minutes beyond our trysting time when I crept out the door onto the cold, dark street. There was no sign of Frank; he had either gone without me or was still snugly wrapped up between the blankets. Fearing for the safety of our catch I decided not to hang around but to go out and do a spell of guard duty. The clammy hand of night still held its grip on the land when I arrived at my destination. I lay against a nearby hedge to await Frank's arrival, though I felt that he had reneged, preferring the comfort of his bed to a vaporous promise of wealth. A few curious stars peeped down from behind the lowering clouds that scurried overhead to see sleep sneak up to reclaim me.

The chill gnawing at my marrow elbowed slumber aside. How long I had lain there I did not know, but dark-ness still prevailed. I lit a fag, more to heat my hands from its warm glow than for the pleasure of smoking. I was beginning to think that old Sol was as idle as Frank and too lazy to get up when I became conscious of the first glimmer of light in the eastern sky. Writing Frank off as a hopeless case I decided to go it alone, and climbed over the five-bar gate into the first field, making my way gingerly along the side of the hedge. I had not gone far when my eyes, fully adjusted to the poor light, fell upon a white blob in the short grass. Bending closer to investigate I discovered it was a rabbit lying dead in a snare. It wasn't one of our snares, that was for sure; there were still two fields to cross before reaching the site of our own traps. We were not the only trappers operating in this area and I had accidently stumbled upon someone else's catch. What was the honourable thing to do in this situation? Leave it to fall into the hands of some unscrupulous thief? Take it into protective custody on behalf of the rightful owner? Having already been warned of the fate that befell poachers I was reluctant to take it in case anybody saw me and misconstrued my intentions. Other, less charitable ideas entered my head; after all, there were two faces to every coin and what if our own traps had failed us? If that happened there would be no pictures tonight, and what was that old saying about a bird in the hand? Praying to the good God above to forgive me, I succumbed to temptation; a true descendant of the two in the Garden. Figuring that I might as well be shot for a sheep as a lamb I pulled the stake out of the ground and made off with both snare and rabbit. A few paces along I came upon another victim of the unknown trapper. All my scruples had by now evaporated and I had no hesitation in acquiring for myself another couple of bob's worth of bunny flesh. With two rabbits dangling from their traps I made my way towards the gap in the hedge ahead, full of the joys of the early morning air.

I had not progressed very far before I became aware of the fact that I had developed a sixth sense; I had an uncanny feeling that I was under observation. I stopped dead in my tracks, a cold fear sending a tingle up my spine; my eyes danced about in their sockets searching for the source of my apprehension. I quickly found it. On the low wall beneath the hedge towards which I was heading, silhouetted against the lightening sky, was what appeared to me to be a human head. It certainly was no stone: I had never seen a stone with protuberances resembling ears before, and I was in no mood to investigate the phenomenon more closely. Nonchalantly, I edged closer to the hedge on my right as if seeking further loot, quietly dropping my booty as I moved. No spectre melted through solid walls as quickly as I did through those dense whitethorn bushes. Emerging on the other side I took off like a bullet from a gun, never slowing down till I was almost home. I was not aware of it at the time but, at about the precise moment of my dematerialization, Frank was making his grand entrance to the arena.

He failed to turn up for school that day and I assumed that he must have taken ill during the night. When he failed to show his face on the street that afternoon my concern for him grew, so I called around to his house to enquire about his health. His mother ushered me into the kitchen. There sat Frank at the table, looking the picture of misery.

He sported a beautiful black eye, a split and swollen upper lip and several other facial abrasions.

"What in the name of God has happened to you?" I enquired.

"You didn't turn up this morning," said he, "so I decided to go and see to the snares myself. I found two rabbits lying on the track in the first field. I had just picked them up when some lunatic attacked me, saying I had stolen his rabbits, that I had taken them and his snares, and honest to God I hadn't."

"I believe you. What I'm sorry about is not being there to help you, but I slept in," said I, lying through my teeth.

The Kid from Durango

THAT MUCH MALIGNED fellow of fig-leaf fame who was so ignominiously chucked out of Eden on the trumped-up charge that he had succumbed to the blandishments of a snake-in-the-grass was not the original sinner we have been brainwashed into believing. His creator, flushed with success at having fashioned Adam from a piece of clay, had grown more ambitious and embarked on an experiment that millenia later would be emulated by the infamous Baron Frankenstein – the creation of life from old bones. On realising that the raw material necessary for his new venture was not readily available the experimenter resorted to vivisection, mugging poor Adam and purloining one of his ribs. A spin-off from this act of wanton violence was the invention of sin. This assault upon his person was a traumatic experience in itself for the unfortunate man but when the rib turned up next day to accost him with demands for a fur coat it was the final straw. He lost control of his faculties completely and in all fairness could no longer be held responsible for his actions. He fell in with bad reptilian company, frequented the lowest dives, caroused late into the night and gradually lost the last vestiges of self-respect. Finally, on reaching the depths of degradation, he turned to devouring Cox's Orange Pippins. For this heinous act he was evicted from home and garden, forced to take his animated rib with him and doomed to spend the rest of his days wandering in the wilderness, struggling to fend for them both.

The legacy that Adam left to mankind was not sin. He left to us a folk-memory, a desire to escape from the realities of life, to regain Eden, to return again to that paradise of which he had been so unjustly deprived. Our cave-dwelling ancestors' quest for the fulfilment of that dream led to their clubbing themselves into insensibility; the modern seeker may resort to drugs, but we were satisfied to lose ourselves among the shadows that flickered across the silvered screen of our local picture palace, addicts to the celluloid productions of the Hollywood dream factories.

There was no caste system in evident existence in our democratic young nation. Nobody bore a red spot on the forehead to distinguish him from his social inferiors. There were some obvious pointers enabling the observant to tell at a glance whether or not the man in the street was affluent or on the verge of destitution, but it was the cinema that provided the best guide to people's financial circumstances. With up to three changes of programme every week in our two halls, only the upper crust could afford regular attendance at the princely sum of one shilling. For the less well-heeled a reasonably comfortable seat in the parterre could be had for eightpence and at the bottom of the social pile fourpence gave one licence to jostle, heave and push onto one of the extremely uncomfortable wooden forms that were the thrones of the "gods".

Segregation began at the door, there being two separate entrances, one shared by the nabobs and fat cats and the other for the exclusive use of the gods. We "gods" entered a foyer that was strictly functional and devoid of all adornment, containing only a pay-desk where we parted with our pennies in exchange for a ticket that was quickly snatched from our hands to be torn in two. Clutching half a ticket we were ushered through swing-doors into a drab, dimly lit passage that led us unerringly to our Shangri-La. The welcome that awaited our eightpenny and shilling betters was of the red-carpet variety. Framed, autographed photographs of leading stars graced the decorated walls and a well-dressed representative of management bestowed nods, smiles or handshakes as considered appropriate before they passed through to their well-upholstered seats.

But whether our money provided us with a wooden form or a plush seat there was one thing we all shared in common – a constant battle with the ubiquitous flea. It was not without good reason that we referred to both of these establishments as "bug-houses". The inspiration for this appellation would become painfully obvious to any stranger that stepped through their doors, new blood being as welcome to these denizens of the dark interiors as a jar of strawberry jam to an undernourished wasp. Each hall had its own unique aroma, giving a clue to the particular brand of pesticide favoured by their respective managements but doing nothing to recommend either poison as a panache offering relief to the patrons' nightly suffering. The family tree of every flea that lived within twenty miles of town had its roots in one or other cinema. A hardy little bunch that defied all efforts at extermination, they were of migratory bent, adventuring far afield with their homegoing hosts, founding new colonies far and wide, their descendants frequently returning to help in replenishing the population of the homelands.

These bloodsucking little hoppers recognised no class barrier; we were all fair game. Where we differed was in how we relieved our discomfort. The gods scratched openly; one always knew who was doing the catering for an unwelcome guest. The eightpennies were more discreet in dislodging their parasitic diners; the unobtrusive crossing or uncrossing of a leg, the slight shift in position as if alleviating cramp or stimulating the circulation; never blatantly scratching, it being considered unbecoming to admit playing host to vermin. How the upper crust coped with these irritating little insects we found difficult to imagine since they were hidden from our view high up in the balcony. Having heard it said on more than one occasion that their philosophy of life was "I'll scratch your back if you'll scratch mine," we reckoned they practised it physically as well as metaphorically.

That our few pennies purchased a couple of hours of pleasure and escapism was undeniable, however poor the show, but for some of us even that miniscule sum would be too much of a price to pay. There was only one thing better than seeing a good picture and that was seeing it for nothing. All our cunning and subterfuge was mustered to achieve that end. The siege of Troy was re-enacted every night but with more clever ploys and ruses than something as outmoded and cumbersome as a wooden horse. The most popular and successful method was to club together to raise enough cash to finance one admission; someone who at the first opportunity would throw open one of the emergency doors and who would be nimble enough to avoid being trampled to death in the ensuing stampede. Clandestine entry and precipitate departure were but two faces of the same coin. When the "Greeks" had breached the defences legitimate young patrons braced themselves for what was to follow. A torchlight beam playing on the face, a few well chosen questions on preceding events on screen and one's fate was sealed. Possession of a ticket was no passport to immunity from expulsion. There was only one criterion upon which judgement would be based: fast and correct answers. Hesitation or failure to satisfy the quizmaster resulted in being dragged out of one's seat by the collar and heaved out on the street like an unruly drunk from a down-town bar. There was no running home to tell the "ma" – it was all considered part of the game.

The dramas and comedies churned out by the Hollywood studios were frequently outrivalled and overshadowed by the antics that periodically erupted among the gods; capers that provided real-life entertainment and which were generally accepted as an extra bonus for our money. An occasional and much appreciated source of amusement was the sudden outburst from a hick on one of his rare visits to the gaff. Having seen some character bumped off in the supporting picture do a Lazarus and reappear bubbling with robust good health in the main feature he would be shaken to the core. Considering himself as having been conned out of his fourpence he would jump from his seat to rant and rave, accusing management of deception and fraud. Having seen somebody killed he expected him to stay dead. Rumour had it that white-coated attendants were employed to subdue such simple Philistines but observation showed that the proprietor had his own enlightened and effective method of resolving these periodic upsets: booting through the door with firm instructions to stay out until sanity and reason returned.

Another wet-nurse to the appreciative of the spontaneous side-show was the handy-lad. The tools of his calling were spanners, screwdrivers or pliers with which he would amuse himself surreptitiously dismantling the seating. Having satisfied himself that he had removed sufficient bolts, screws or nails he would slink off to a safe distance to await the inevitable collapse and to join in the chorus of applause and uproarious cheers that unfailingly greeted the undignified heap of limb-flailing bodies sprawling on the floor.

The fist fight was the most common form of diversion and undoubtedly the most popular. A vicious no-holds-barred fight would break out for the most trivial of reasons: an imagined slight, an obstructed view or the disputed right to a few square inches of seating. The attraction to the scene of combat would be magnetic. Scaling over seats and each other the gods would converge for a close-up of the action with the outcome being the disappearance of the protagonists as they drowned in a sea of screaming, blood-lusting fight fans.

Those were the golden days of the film industry and the moguls took full advantage of the fact, producing their visual fantasies almost as prolifically as Henry Ford manufactured cars and with a quality equally as variable. Ownership of a cinema was as lucrative as access to a pathway to rainbow's end. Full houses were practically guaranteed, though there was slight fluctuation through the week like the ebbing and flowing of the tide. Its lowest ebb on Wednesday reflected the financial circumstances of the majority of regulars, but gathering momentum towards the week-end on Sunday night it reached full flow.

This was the night when the wooden forms groaned and creaked in protest beneath the pressure of two-tier occupancy. With air-conditioning an unknown luxury perspiration would flow copiously as temperatures soared to fever pitch. The vapours rising from the tightly packed mass of humanity, intermingling with the malodorous reek of unwashed bodies, sweaty feet and the furtive emissions of the wind-breaking bacon and cabbage brigade scattered strategically throughout the pit, created an atmosphere reminiscent of the farmyard manure heap. We endured conditions for which Calcutta and its Black Hole had become infamous, gaining such masochistic pleasure from the experience that there were many who would have sold their souls rather than miss out.

Some films of those years have stood the test of time and are still screened as epics of the art, milestones in the careers of the actors who starred in them. Henry Fonda's *Grapes of Wrath*, James Cagney's *Angels with Dirty Faces*, Mickey Rooney's *Boys Town* and many, many more. Good as these films were, the picture of which I have the most vivid memory was no masterpiece but a mediocrity from one of Hollywood's Poverty Row studios probably handed out to exhibitors as cigarette cards were supplied to smokers.

It featured that all-American boy, the "Durango Kid" himself — Charles Starrett.

It was the night my brother entertained the notion that he was now ᴏld enough to graduate from the matinée scene and join me on an evening excursion for my fix. His tears and plaintive wails penetrated to our father's heart and moved him to sacrifice a few pipes of tobacco by putting a shilling in my hand. It was a shilling with a string attached: Cinderella could go to the ball but would have to be back in the house before the clock struck nine.

To have escaped from that bedlam called matinée and take his place among adults was a thrill beyond measure to the little lad. When the lights dimmed and the credits rolled for the first of the two pictures he was transported in thrall into the make-believe world of the cowboys where white-stetsoned Starrett, the epitome of Western bravura and chivalry, was cleaning up yet another town, routing baddies and winning the admiration and love of the fair maid. My brother was captivated; he had found in the "Durango Kid" a new hero. Clutching at imaginary reins he rode his phantom steed beside the Lionheart of the range, his fists flaying the air in forlorn hopes of downing bad guys. His screams of warning and encouragement rent the air and assaulted the ear. The more animated his behaviour and clamorous his exhortations the further I slunk in my seat, cowering in embarrassment.

I offered up thanks to God as the "Kid" rode off into the sunset and the picture faded from the screen, little knowing that worse was to come. The brother showed no interest in the main feature; he had remained behind in the land of "Howdy pard" and sagebrush. As if afflicted with a severe attack of St. Vitus's dance compounded by verbal haemorrhage he relived the previous picture scene by scene. Among calls and pleas to gag or remove him I borrowed a leaf from the apostle Peter's book and feebly denied I knew my own brother, fooling nobody but myself.

When the lights went up I rose to leave but was jerked back into my seat by a sharp tug on my jacket.

"Can't we just see a little bit of the cowboy picture again?"

Always a soft touch and a sucker for punishment, against my better judgement I agreed. "Five minutes only, then we're going home."

"Can't we just see that bit where he jumped off his horse onto the bad guy?"

"Can't we just see the stampede?"

"Can't we just . . . ?"

We saw the whole picture through a second time. When we tumbled out onto the street it had long gone ten o'clock. There would be no riding home in a golden coach for Cinders tonight but one mad dash to put Einstein's theories on time and motion to a practical test. Somewhere along the line that eminent young man of science had got his figures wrong because when we finally charged through the kitchen door time had done a quickstep and beaten us. Moments later I was packed off to bed smarting from the stings that made me kindred spirit to the saddle-sore cowboy, but burning deep within me was a bitter and lasting enmity towards Charles Starrett and the Kid from Durango.

The High Flyer

OUTSIDE OF THE annual and festive holidays there was only one other event that guaranteed me a regular, officially approved escape from tutorial confinement and that was on the day that Duffy's circus came to town. There might be some other unexpected breaks to rejoice in, like election day, but these were so unpredictable and infrequent that they could be discounted. Duffy, however, was as dependable as the seasons and I was always pleased to see the billposters pasting up the notices of his imminent arrival. I could never lay claim to having ever been a dedicated circus fan; all I was really interested in was the half-holiday that I might squeeze out of its one-day visit. I sometimes found myself with a ringside seat but it was a privilege that owed more to the whims of the gods than the graciousness of my mother; if she had a tanner in her purse by the middle of the week it would be very unlikely to find its way into Mister Duffy's pocket.

When the first of the wagons rolled into town I was more often than not wandering through Dreamland, but as I sluggishly dragged my feet in the direction of school I might just witness the arrival of the latecomers, garishly decked out, and emblazoned on all sides with the name that was synonymous with circus – Duffy.

Opening schools on circus day was an exercise in futility, there being no room for learning in minds that were

filled to overflowing with thoughts of animals and acro-
bats. In the early afternoon a forest of arms would spring
up in response to the teacher's enquiry as to how many
intended to go to the matinée. My hand was always among
the first in the air and more often than not I was first out
the door, though I knew I had a far better chance of taking
off on a flight to Mars than wringing the sixpence admission fee out of my mother.

Fleetness of foot was paramount if one was to be sure of
a good position on the wall surrounding the fair field in
which the big top had been erected. Like the birds that
lined up on the overhead wires preparatory to migration,
we straddled the wall as dangerously threatening to John
Duffy's profits as a flock of rooks to a farmer's corn. For
the men who had been on the road since before dawn, and
who had prepared the site for the big show, there was to be
no rest; they were now ranged in battle order, armed with
sticks and cudgels in defence of their master's smackers.
Were it not for constant vigilance the artistes could very
well have found themselves playing to a full house without
a copper having entered the coffers. There were three lines
of defence, the first patrolling up and down just inside the
wall, occasionally lashing out with their weapons in an
attempt to dislodge us. The second line circled the outer
edge of the big top brandishing switches that frequently
made painful contact with the rear end of an advance
guard of the besieging forces trying to wriggle beneath the
canvas. The third line patrolled within the fortress and
was by far the most feared. Once one had outwitted the
outer brigades they were no longer a threat and could be
forgotten, but if one were lucky enough to secure a seat
the danger remained right through the show of being
approached and requested to produce a ticket, and failure
to comply could prove to be a more painfully prolonged
ordeal than being thrown to the lions. I did manage to
wangle myself a seat once or twice but never considered

the entertainment worth risking my hide and most certainly not worth sixpence.

When the news broke that another type of circus was coming to town the place was agog with excitement; it was to be something entirely new, having never before been even dreamed of. Some posh Englishman by the name of Sir Alan Cobham was to pay us a visit and to bring with him the latest idea in modern entertainment – an air circus. The posters announcing the coming event drew as much attention as if they were proclaiming the second coming of the Messiah. If the promises were anything to go by the traditional circus had had its day and John Duffy was in line for the workhouse. We would see things that previously we had only seen on the screen: stunt flying, wing-walkers, parachutists and, for good measure, for those who could afford it, sightseeing flights over the town. In those days to see an aeroplane at all was such a rarity that when one did appear people flocked out of doors and craned their necks to look and to marvel at the wondrous works of modern man. Thanks to Hollywood everybody was familiar with flight, and pictures that featured aircraft and aerial battles were as popular as cowboys. To the younger generation of the day "Tail-spin Tommy" was the hero of the hour as he daringly defied death in his weekly serial, but seeing dare-devils in the flesh and to have the opportunity of watching their aerial antics in reality was a prospect that fired the imagination.

The racecourse was the venue for the great display and for once the weather held fair bringing out the crowds in their thousands. The road from town was choked with cars and pedestrians in a good-humoured exodus. There was no furtiveness or cloak and dagger approach on my part that day; it was a family outing and even my mother, who normally stayed at home to hold the fort, was not going to miss this one. There was a carnival atmosphere in the warm air as we mingled with the happy crowd that stood or lay about on the green and cooling grass waiting for the show to open. Pedlars of ice-cream, lemonade and a host of other refreshments raked in the lolly from the teeming mass of pleasure-seeking spendthrifts, some of whom, on the morrow, would be scratching about trying to scrape up the price of a loaf of bread.

The roar of the engines that wafted across from the far side of the field where the machines were being tuned up added to the sense of excitement and expectancy. The show got off to a flying start when the squadron of assorted machines took to the air and passed low overhead in an opening salute. From the heavy, twin-engined, passenger-carrying biplane to the wondrous, wingless autogiro, we were treated to a mass demonstration of aeronautical effi-cacy that left one in no doubt about the quality of the men and the safety of the machines. It was an opening that instilled confidence in the crowd and paid dividends to the aeronauts; fears and trepidations were dispelled, resulting in long queues of converts to the flight on which they hoped to get airborne. For the majority it was the sedate, ten minute flip over the town and the bay, while the more daring risked the loop-the-loop in a twin-seater, open-cock-pit monoplane. Screams of apprehension and pleasure could be heard above the noise of the engines as planes zoomed within feet of the ground before soaring into the sky in a spectacular awe-inspiring loop. Wing-walkers and parachutists were everything and more than we had been promised, making it a day to be remembered, and nobody, not even those that trooped home penniless, could say other than that they had got value for money.

There was only one small hitch to the day's events and unfortunately for my father it was to rob him of his one and only opportunity of going up in an aircraft. For years he had harboured an ambition to soar above the clouds, to be one of the élite that could boast of having been "up". From the first moment he had heard of the forthcoming air circus he sacrificed one of his few pleasures in life – his Saturday pint – to save the money to satisfy his dream. He was one of the long queue which waited patiently and excitedly for a seat in the largest of the winged pleasure craft and was bubbling with exhilaration as he took his seat and the plane taxied out for take-off. Whether he was fortunate or downright unlucky is debatable. He never got his flight but, on the other hand, neither did he lose his life. In the first few yards of the run-up to take-off the undercarriage collapsed and brought the plane to an abrupt halt as it ploughed deep furrows in the grassy runway, sending shock waves through the watching crowd and severely shaking the occupants. How disastrous the outcome might have been if the mishap had occurred only seconds later or at the moment of touch-down did not bear contemplation, but all that troubled my father when he rejoined the family was his disappointment at not making it into the wide, blue yonder.

Not only did that plane come close to ending my father's life, but by a peculiar twist of fate was indirectly instrumental in the near termination of my own. It was several weeks before the damage was repaired and it took off again to rejoin the circus somewhere up-country, weeks in which it and its retinue of repair men had been a focus for the curious. Among the gawpers and gogglers that trooped regularly to the site were some of the bigger lads of our street. Several years older than our gang and thirsting for adventures beyond the mundane, their imaginations were fired by the derring-do of Cobham and his fellow aviators. Their hearts were now set on dabbling in the mechanics of flight and their ambition was to construct their own aircraft. Their sights were not set on anything as sophisticated as the craft they had seen at the air circus; for one thing, aero engines were in short supply in our neck of the woods and for another there was the problem of transportation from the site of manufacture to a suitable runway. After several conferences and a great deal of deliberation they settled for a glider.

While they were still in the planning stages we younger ones were also concentrating on aerial problems, though our experiments were concerned more with happy landings. Enthralled with the parachutists, for weeks we concentrated on developing our own. Potato- and flour-sacks, string, rope and fine wire were collected and woven into various designs in the search for success, and how necks and limbs were not broken in foolhardy leaps from high walls and ruined buildings was a miracle. Sprains and abrasions neared epidemic proportions, and were it not for getting wind of the other project and chucking the towel in on our own misguided trials one of us could have ended up with a resting place beneath mother earth rather than the hoped-for soft landing on it.

The hours spent by our bigger neighbours out at the racecourse were paying dividends; picking the brains of the mechanics was enlightening them on the practicalities of aeronautics. They talked knowingly of such things as ailerons, flaps and tail-planes; there were heated discussions on such mysterious subjects as lift and drag that left us younger ones bewildered as they debated the advantages of struts over stress. Construction got under way in the confines of the disused quarry in the old gaol. No plans had been drawn up, and as each lad had his own idea on size and method of construction it looked like the whole project would collapse before getting off the ground. Watching the capers from the vantage-point of the quarry edge was akin to having a balcony seat at a Laurel and Hardy picture as the craftsmen quarrelled and squabbled, alternating between construction and destruction. Slowly and unsurely, out of the chaos and confusion came forth progress, and a flimsy wooden framework looking like a small-scale skeleton of a circus biplane appeared.

Though a long way from completion it did look promising, and we who had sat to scoff and ridicule came down from our lofty perch and offered our services in the hope of sharing in the glory. We were considered to be worthless, except as scroungers and scavengers to scour the district for material to cover the frame, and our masters would be satisfied with nothing less than the best flour-sacks. The fine weave of the flour-sack, we were informed, would be more acceptable to the tar with which they intended to finish off their handiwork, and that tar we would have to risk pinching from the council depot.

Sitting on its undercarriage of perambulator wheels, the black, streamlined contraption looked as if it could be wafted away on a zephyr. It was Frank who threw the spanner in the works.

"Who's going to fly it?" he asked innocently.

With all the planning and hard work nobody had considered such a minor detail as making provision for a pilot. There was no going back to the drawing-board because there had never been one to start with, so thinking caps had to be shook out and donned. It was the modern equivalent of the chicken and egg problem: did they fashion a cockpit and find a pilot to fit, or find a pilot and fashion a cockpit to suit? They arrived at the conclusion that it would be more sensible to find someone daft enough to take the job, and all eyes turned on me. It was not so much that I was looked upon as light in the head as that I was light in stature. Lack of weight was the overriding factor in their considerations; that it coincided with lack of sense just happened to be the luck of the draw. They had made a slight misjudgement; I was not going to be catapulted into the air without putting up some semblance of a fight.

"I'm not going up in that," I protested.

"Why not? Sure 'twill be a marvellous experience."

"'Cos I like it here on the ground, that's why."

"Don't you want to be famous like Blearyeyed?" I heard

someone ask.

"Who's Blearyeyed? Never heard of him," I replied.

"He was that French fella that flew the English Channel. It made him a hero."

"Send for him then. I don't want to be a hero, I'm not doing it."

"Ah, he's yellow," came the snide remark.

That got my goat. I wasn't going to have a yellow label tagged onto me.

"All right, I'll do it," I blurted out. "But I want paying, I want half a dollar."

I thought that by pitching my price so high I would put an end to the matter, but I had underestimated their enthusiasm. They moved away and went into a huddle then returned with four tanners and six pennies. I was committed.

Modifications began immediately and took several days to complete. The biggest hurdle was the installation of controls, which in the end turned out to be nothing more sophisticated than several wires leading from two bars in the cockpit to the tail-end of the craft – wires on which my fate would depend.

On the day of the proposed launch I suffered such an attack of cold feet they were in danger of becoming frost-bitten, and I desperately sought a way out without losing face. I thought I had hit on the ideal solution when I demanded a flying suit. I was wrong. In a flash one of my more resourceful patrons was off down the field and returned a few minutes later with a leather coat and cap and a pair of goggles belonging to his motor-cyclist broth-er. The coat and cap were several sizes too large but with some skilful wrapping and packing were rendered accept-able. There was a little more difficulty with the goggles and no matter how well they were adjusted I felt like Ben Turpin, the cross-eyed screen comic, as I peeped out around the inner edges of the rims. I now looked as daft as

I knew I was behaving.

The news of my daring attempt at unpowered flight had spread like wildfire around the neighbourhood and had attracted nearly as many spectators as one would expect to find at a football final. I had a brief lecture about thermals, downdraughts and updraughts before glider and I were raised shoulder high and swept away to the grassy slope that led down to the quarry edge. If I had tried to escape I would have had no chance: quicker than I could grasp what was happening I was bundled into the cockpit, pointed in the appropriate direction and pushed at high speed down the hill towards death or glory. Just a moment before I was hurtled into space I caught a glimpse of my mother, closely followed by Frank, racing up the field waving her arms in terror.

Whether out of jealousy or concern for my well-being Frank had rushed off at the last minute to inform her that I was intent on making aviation history. He needn't have bothered: the attempt was a disaster. Weeks of dedication and hard work were wasted as the craft and its heroic occupant took a nose-dive down the craggy rock-face. It tumbled and twisted, bouncing and bumping from rock to rock down the thirty-foot drop, breaking into several pieces before throwing me roughly on to my behind on a clump of grass. For a split second I remained sitting upright, then rolled over backward, the back of my skull making violent contact with a jagged rock that jutted out of the ground. If I were to say that I was killed I would be branding myself a barefaced liar, but what I can say is that the multitude of multi-coloured stars I saw bore no resemblance to anything I had ever before seen on this earth. I opened my eyes to see a host of curious faces peering down from the top of the cliff. I remembered the glimpse I had got of my mother in the moment before my plummet and hastily jumped to my feet just in time to see her elbow her way through the crowd of onlookers. I raised my hand to rub the back of my head and found that the leather cap had been pierced. I removed it to find the inside stained with blood, not a great deal but enough to let me know that I had wound up with more than a lump on the bonce. I put it down as just another graze and prepared myself to face the music of maternal reproof.

Surprisingly I received none. Her anger was directed against those whom she considered should have had more sense, though she did order confinement to barracks. Unwilling to let her see that I had been injured I confined myself to my bedroom until she calmed down sufficiently for me to dare ask to be allowed out. It was to Frank I went with my tale of woe and asked him to survey the damage.

"Your head's split open," he said, "though it's not bleeding very much. I think you'd better have something on it."

Soon all the gang knew, and with oohs and aahs informed me that they could see my brains.

"You'd better go to the chemist and get some iodine on it," suggested Gerald. "It might go septic."

Like a wounded soldier to a dressing station I was led away to the nearest chemist shop where, for a penny, I had it painted with a liberal dollop of stinging iodine and covered with sticking plaster. The plaster would not stick; the harder it was pressed down the higher it bounced back. The chemist was a man who would not easily admit defeat and having accepted my money was determined to give value. He came at me with a cut-throat razor, hacked a lump of hair off and shaved me to the scalp, yet still the plaster refused to lie down.

"Must be a faulty plaster," he consoled himself. "We sometimes get the odd one."

He washed my skull with spirits and tried a new plaster – without success; it was as stubborn as the first one. I thought he might have to nail it down or give up in despair, but he had another solution – a roll of bandage.

My mother nearly fell off her chair in shock when I walked through the door in my new turban.

"What in the name of God have you been up to now?" she cried.

"Oh, it's nothing," I tried to console her. "The plaster wouldn't stick to that cut I got this morning, so the chemist had to put a bandage on. I'll be all right."

"What cut? I didn't know you cut yourself."

"I didn't want to worry you; anyway, it's only a nick."

That was the understatement of the year. The following morning my mother removed the bandage and plaster to have a look for herself and was shaken by what she saw. It was no nick, but a nasty looking gash.

"Are you sure you feel all right?" she asked concernedly.

"Just a bit sore, that's all," I assured her.

Washing the wound and dressing it with ointment and lint, she replaced the bandage and insisted that there would be no more school for me until it had healed up. I had no objection to being kept home from school but when she forbade me from going out to play I felt rather cheated. While it was a pleasure to lie in bed and listen to the others preparing for school, when they returned home, had a meal and hurried out to enjoy themselves I felt like a wild animal might do when confined to a cage. Thinking it would all be over in a few days, I was more than surprised when at the end of a week my mother remarked that it was beginning to look rather nasty; it was showing signs of pus and tending to swell.

The daily dressings with different brands of ointments were to no avail and it looked as if the doctor would have to be called in before the condition of the wound deteriorated any further and turned gangrenous. There was only one treatment for that condition and I saw no future for me as an amputee. As things turned out it never came to that, and neither did we require the services of the medical practitioner. My mother abandoned proprietary cure-alls and pinned her faith on an "old reliable" – the hot bread and water fomentation. The result was nothing short of miraculous. From the first application improvement was noticeable; the pus and poisons were sucked out and the surrounding tissue took on a healthy glow. Within a couple of weeks the scalp had healed and the hair began to sprout, and I would never have shown sign of injury if it were not for the hollow.

What had caused so much trouble and worry was more than a flesh-wound; I had lost a piece of my skull. Whether it had been gouged out or pushed in I don't know to this day, but I do know that if I am ever caught out in the rain there is a built-in receptacle in my nut, a permanent reminder of Sir Alan Cobham and his aviation-inspiring circus.

The Big Fellow

EVERY TIME I met him on the street I crossed over to the other side or slipped into the nearest shop. I was scared of him and had good reason to be: he was big and burly and I was his "public enemy number one". I had not been aware of the man's existence and probably never would have been had I not descended into the underworld to become counterfeiter, arsonist and suspected subversive.

It had all begun innocently enough and little did I realise as I walked through the shop door with the fake coin in my hand what a thorn in the flesh I was to become to this big arm of the law. It was a copper coin that had been dipped in a mercury solution and as a result had acquired a silvery sheen, and to the unwary it could be mistaken for a coin of higher value. My mistake was in thinking that anybody wearing what looked remarkably like milk-bottle bottoms as a substitute for spectacles must be either blind or extremely stupid. The victim of my intended swindle was neither, though she did make one mistake – she parted with the Woodbines I had asked for before picking my dud money from the counter. The moment her sensitive fingers made contact the game was up. I vacated the premises in double-quick style with threats of her having the law on me ringing in my ears.

"The headmaster wants to see you immediately," said the teacher as he entered the classroom.

"What the hell does the doddering old fool want with me?" I thought as I tapped nervously on his office door.

I had guessed the answer to that question before I reached his desk. The two strangers with whom he was engaged in small-talk needed no introduction: I could tell at a glance what their occupations were and the nature of their business. Old four-eyes had been true to her word and had informed the law on my previous day's attempted fraudulent transaction.

"We would like ye to accompany us to de barricks," said the bigger of the two. "Dere's a little matter of tryin' to pass funny munney, and we tink ye mite be able to help us wit our enquiries."

Scared though I was at what might befall me when they had me down at their headquarters, it crossed my mind as he took me by the elbow and led me out onto the street that I was in the iron grip of a Corkman. With that peculiarity of speech for which the tribes of our neighbouring county were noted there was no mistaking the well-spring of his nativity.

Flanked by the two I was frog-marched through town attracting curious glances from the passing throng. Through the corner of my eye I caught a glimpse of Danny slinking like a sidewinder up a back street. Luxuriating in one of his rest-from-school days he had no intention of having it marred by being roped in to any skulduggery his pal was involved in.

"In dere," said the Big Fellow as he pushed me through the doorway of a large room. "Impty yer pockets."

There wasn't much to empty: a few crumpled butt-ends, a couple of loose matches, a sticky sweet that had wrapped itself in a fluffy coat, a length of string and a rusty penknife that I had picked out of the gutter that very morning. From the look of disappointment on his face I was relieved to think that nothing I had on my person could be classified as incriminating evidence.

"Sit down dere and wait," he said, indicating an uncomfortable looking straight-backed chair by the large table on which my treasured possessions had been spread. He left the room and a moment later a young uniformed man entered and asked if I would like a cup of tea. He sat with me as I sipped and waited for the Big Fellow's return. It was a long wait but the time wasn't wasted. I learned a few things that might be of advantage to me when my grilling would begin. I gathered that the Corkman's name was O'Hooligan and that he could be a very hard man but that he had a heart of pure gold for those who were cooperative, that he had influence with people in high places and that he could fix it for me to get away with a light sentence if I made life easy for him by coming clean and making a full confession about my plans to undermine the financial stability of the state.

Looking like the cat that had swallowed the cream O'Hooligan charged through the door clutching a brown paper bag in his ham-like fist. He emptied its contents on the table before me.

"What ye got to say about dis den?"

Strewn across the table were about a dozen coin-shaped pieces of lead.

"They're pieces of lead," I replied quickly, hoping to impress him with my knowledge of metallurgy.

"A wise-guy are ye? Well let me tell ye de're kines."

"De're not kines, de're pieces of lead," I said in my best imitation of the Cork accent.

"Don't git funny wit me or ye'll never git out of here," his heavy jowls clouded with frustration and anger. "De're kines an' ye made dem; we searched yer house and found dem. What ye got to say fer yerself now den?"

I found it hard to believe, but it was true, as I was to learn later. Accompanied by a couple of uniformed men he had barged in on my mother armed with a warrant to search the house. He had probed through every nook and cranny; even the beds were stripped in his paranoid determination to build up evidence against me as a big-time counterfeiter. His only success had been a few pieces of lead that I had shaped for my sister and her friends to play "shops" with. Not much, but it was enough for this cretin to convince himself that he had got his hands on a master criminal. I had a sneaking feeling that I was in deep trouble and that maybe I should take a leaf from the Hollywood gangsters' book and demand to see my lawyer. The only trouble was I didn't have one.

"We've got plenty on ye. Ye'd better make a statement an' let us know who else is in on it."

Then he dropped his bombshell.

"I tink 'tis only fair to tell ye Dublin Castle knows about ye, de're sendin' a Special Branch man down to question ye."

I felt myself break out in a cold sweat. I had visions of Scotland Yard and the FBI being called in; I could see myself taking the rap for every unsolved case of counterfeiting on international police files. I would soon be in the same league as Al Capone, and all for five Woodbines.

The evidence against me was a statement from the dim-sighted shopkeeper coupled with what was laid out on the table: twelve pieces of lead and the fateful coin which still bore traces of doctoring. It didn't look much to me but O'Hooligan seemed to look upon it as his ticket to promotion. He was on his way up the ladder and I was but one of the rungs.

"I've bin patient wit ye lad; don't make me git rough. Jist let me have a confession, dat's all I want."

Before I could open my mouth the door opened to admit a smartly uniformed Inspector. He looked from me to the junk on the table before turning to O'Hooligan to enquire what was going on.

"I've caught a counterfeiter, sur," said the Big Fellow, "he's jist about to make a statement dat he's responsible fer all dese fake kines dat's floatin' about."

"Is this the evidence?" queried the Inspector as he ran his index finger through the bits of lead.

"'Tis sur, dat's it," replied O'Hooligan, shoulders back, chest expanded and his face beaming with pride.

"Come with me a moment," said the Inspector as he moved towards the door.

It had hardly closed behind them when I heard the Inspector's voice raised in angry remonstration. O'Hooligan was being torn off a strip for wasting police time on a triviality. As I strained my ears to catch what was being said I learned that the Inspector had not reached his exalted position in the force without knowing the difference between "kines" and pieces of lead.

Stepping out of the door a free man I knew exactly how to play the part of a guy who had just beaten the rap. Stuffing a stub in the corner of my mouth I struck a match on the nearby wall, slowly lit up, stepped out onto the pavement, hitched my trousers with both elbows and strutted up the street. Glancing over my shoulder as I moved away I saw the Big Fellow watching me from the charge-room window. Caution would have to be my watchword from here on out. That he was smarting from the drubbing he had just received from his superior was crystal clear: vengeance was burning in his eyes.

I was a nine-day wonder with the lads as I told, re-told, elaborated on and exaggerated my experiences in the hands of the master sleuth, but with the passing of the days I reverted once again to being a nonentity to all except O'Hooligan. He rivalled the Almighty with his omnipresence. There was no escape from him even in my sleep; he invaded my dreams and I would wake up in a cold sweat expecting to find him standing at the foot of the bed. The only place where I could feel free from the all-seeing eye was out of town, so I took to spending my free time out at Danny's place, slowly degenerating into a semi-rustic recluse.

My tactics might have shaken him off my back eventually had I not accidentally landed myself in trouble yet again. I had spent Saturday helping Danny with his weekly chores, giving advice and encouragement from the comfort of the seat in the sun outside his front door. A strenuous day merited a relaxing evening at the pictures. Refreshed by afternoon tea we took a leisurely stroll towards town. The hot tarmac beneath our feet and the humidity in the still air combined to squeeze from our bodies the little energy remaining after a busy day. Throwing ourselves onto a grassy bank we lay back and fished out our butt-ends. Lighting up, I nonchalantly flicked the spent match over my shoulder and relaxed to savour the few puffs I hoped to extract from the short stub.

The cloud of blue smoke that wafted up my nostrils bore no resemblance in aroma or density to what one would expect of finest Virginia tobacco. I jumped up to see a young fire grazing avidly along the bank-top. Our fight to prevent its growth was short-lived. When it reached out a greedy tongue to make a tasty meal of a nearby gorse bush we decided to throw in the towel and beat a hasty retreat.

Walls are reputed to have ears but country hedges certainly have eyes, and our hotfoot departure from the scene of the fiery feast did not pass unnoticed. A local farmer, his attention drawn by the cloud of billowing smoke, caught a glimpse of our fleeing figures and recognised Danny.

With his trouser-bottoms firmly bound to his ankles by a pair of bicycle clips the uniformed guardian of law and order was ushered into the room by my distraught looking mother.

"I've got a summons for you here young man. You'll find it more exciting reading than that *Hotspur*."

"What am I supposed to have done?"

"Read it and see; it seems to me you've been having a scorching time of it."

Trembling like an aspen leaf I took the document from his hand. I was to appear in court on some very serious counts. I had knowingly and maliciously set fire to the hedges, trees and crops of a certain farmer. I had endangered his home and outhouses; furthermore, I had put in jeopardy the lives of himself, his family and livestock. It appeared that I was the perpetrator of the greatest conflagration since the Great Fire of London.

"Who said I had anything to do with that lot?" I asked, vainly trying to hide my trepidation behind a transparent mask.

"Your pal. He was recognised running away from the blaze; he's confessed all. As a matter of fact, he said it was you who were really responsible."

So Judas Iscariot had not died without issue. I had the misfortune to choose as a pal a direct descendant, a chip off the old block who would betray me for even less than his ancestor had betrayed his holy crony. Our companionship was ended. I never wanted to set eyes on him again. When this was all over and I had served my sentence I would move to the Antipodes, or perhaps with a bit of luck I might discover some place even farther away from the miserable wretch. I did not see him again until the morning of the hearing when we came face to face on the courthouse steps. He looked so sheepish that I expected to hear him bleat.

I tried to avoid him as if he were a leper but was halted in my tracks by the sight of the Big Fellow standing by the entrance. Danny, misinterpreting my hesitation, began to ladle apologetic regrets into my unreceptive ear. My interest was focused on the grin that cracked the face of my arch-enemy. He had come to gloat, to witness my imminent departure on a trip up the river. This would be a red-letter day in his flat-foot career.

Taking my seat between Danny and my long-suffering mother I was oblivious to everything that transpired about me. My mind was engrossed with important matters; now was the time to prepare plans for my break from the Big House and it was to the cinema that I turned for inspiration. I did a stretch with Humphrey Bogart in *San Quentin*, I strung along with Paul Muni as *A Fugitive From a Chain Gang* and was starting out with Spencer Tracy to do *Twenty Thousand Years in Sing-Sing* when I was roused from my reveries on hearing my name called by the clerk of the court as he read out the charges against me.

The farmer was first to take the stand. He was asked to identify us and to give an account of the extent of the damage done to his property. With shoulders hunched and features drawn he looked a broken man. Faltering with emotion he explained how he had struggled through the years to wrest a living from the land; how he had valiantly fought off the depredations of all manner of pest and vermin and how he was now on the verge of total destitution because of two rampaging fire-bugs who had put his beloved farm to the torch. By the time he had ceased his whingeing and whining my innards had deserted me and high-tailed it through the door hard on the heels of any frail hopes of freedom I might still have harboured. It was a couple of stilted jellies that made their way to the stand to account for their pyromaniac behaviour.

Our futures were now in the hands of a man whose orchard we had frequently and ruthlessly plundered. He sat like a god upon his throne gazing down on us over the top of his glasses, silently studying us as if we were a couple of lice that had just crawled out of the woodwork. Having finally decided that we might after all be members of the human race, the great Solomon spoke.

"What have you got to say for yourselves then? We're waiting for an explanation."

I felt that it would take the Wizard of Oz to restore to me the courage to speak, so with a nudge of my elbow I delegated Danny to do the honours.

"We're sorry, sir," said Danny.

"So you are sorry are you? Sorry for what? Being caught?"

"Sorry for the fire, sir."

"No need to feel sorry for the fire, it doesn't need your sympathy; it's that poor man you should feel sorry for."

I stole a glance at the victim of our incineration. He was still hamming it up, working on his act as if he were a film star striving to win an Oscar nomination, an honour that would prove to be our nemesis. His John Barrymore histrionics had a dramatic effect upon me; I scraped around within and found I still possessed enough moral fibre to help me speak up and explain by telling the truth, the whole truth and nothing but the truth. My speech from the dock never made the headlines but it had the desired effect upon the court.

"I feel that what you have just told me is an honest account of what transpired," said Solomon after due deliberation, "but I must warn you that to wander about the countryside throwing matchsticks and cigarette-ends around is both stupid and dangerous. Never let me see either of you here again. I'm letting you off with a caution. You may go."

"I swear I'll never raid that man's orchard again," I remarked to Danny as we stepped out into the fresh air and stood on top of the steps to await my mother.

"At least not this year," I continued by way of afterthought.

"He's earned a bit of a break for letting us off so lightly," agreed Danny, "another man would have thrown the book at us. I think I'll give it a rest myself just to show my appreciation."

"I've never been so ashamed in my life," said my mother as she made her appearance. "It's the last time I ever want to see the inside of that place."

We turned to descend to the street when the heavy hand of doom fell on my shoulder.

"Could I have a few words wit ye lads," said the Corkman.

"What about?"

"Jist a few details to clear up, it won't take long."

"All right, what do you want to know?"

"Not here lads. Down at de barricks."

With her inbuilt maternal instincts my mother had caught the scent of a fox. "There is nothing for you to ask, they have been let off. 'Tis all over."

"Oh, 'tis ma'am, I know dat, we jist want to tie up a few loose ends. We won't keep dem long."

Against her better judgement she relented on being assured it was a routine formality.

He was civility personified as he strode between us down the street to the barracks.

"Ye were lucky dere lads, he wint very light on ye. I taut ye'd have a heavy fine at least. 'Twas a serious offence."

By the time we had reached our destination his banter had convinced me that I had seriously misjudged the man: I was beginning to entertain the idea that he might actually have a mother somewhere in Cork; a little old lady pining for her exiled son down here among the mountainy men. Such magnanimous ideas evaporated the moment we entered the building. What had been a nice Dr Jekyll was transformed into a raging Mr Hyde the moment we stepped through the portals.

"In dere, ye," he roared as he bundled me through the doorway of the room I had become so familiar with during the great "kines" investigation, at the same time grabbing Danny by the scruff of the neck and dragging him through to another room.

I settled myself on the old familiar chair and ransacked my memory bank in an effort to find a clue to what charred or smouldering ends we might have left lying about that were of such moment to O'Hooligan. Was it possible that Danny had been engaged in some other skulduggery and had again implicated me? Had I taken to sleepwalking and unknowingly embarked on an orgy of wrong-doing? Such speculation was pointless. I would just have to sit, twiddle my thumbs and amuse myself by counting the knots in the grimy floorboards while I awaited the barbarian's return. Time shambled slowly along: sleep hammered a wedge into my thoughts, scattering them numb and stupefied within the confines of my brainbox. Folding my arms on the table I cradled my head and embarked on a trip to Nod. My pleasant journey was terminated abruptly by the sound of that now-familiar voice.

"It didn't take long to git a confession out o' dat fellow. Now I want yeer story: ye'd better start talkin'."

"Talking about what? What are you talking about?"

"Ye know what I'm talkin' about. Yer pal is an IRA man, dat's what. 'Twas him put de lights out in town last week; ye know all about it."

I knew about the blackout all right. Who didn't? The whole town had been plunged into darkness, but this was the first inkling I had that it was an act of sabotage.

Suddenly I saw the light; I quickly figured out his line of thought: if we were capable of illuminating the countryside we were equally capable of engulfing the town in Stygian gloom. His brilliance dazzled me; genius such as this was wasted in a small town. Our gain was Interpol's loss.

Coming up behind me he grabbed my wrist and twisted my arm up my back. The pain was excruciating and tears welled up in my eyes as I begged for mercy.

"I can have ye locked up without trial for being a member of the IRA, so come on, spill de beans."

His Jekyll personality struggled to the surface and I felt his grip relax to leave a host of pins-and-needles dancing a wild jig up and down my arm. Pulling a packet of Players from his pocket he threw them on the table.

"Go on, have yourself a smoke. Ye're not a bad lad really: 'tis jist ye keep bad company; dat pal of yers downstairs is a real tearaway; he's goin' where he won't be any more trouble."

"What are you going to do with him?"

"He'll be in the Curragh before mornin', 'twill be a long time before we see dat fella agin. He won't want te go alone I can tell ye; he'll try te drag ye wit him; I know his type, sure didn't he shop ye about de fire. My advice is git in first, tell us all ye know about him an' I'll see ye right."

It was an invitation to become a squealer, a copper's nark, to sell Danny down the river. He was making a bad mistake with that offer; I was not to be bought just like that. I would never stoop to betrayal on the strength of a promise. My principles were of more worth than that – at the very least twenty Players and the price of the pictures.

"Ye can have a little time te tink about it; be sure ye have de right answers whin I git back."

There was no improvement on his offer when he did return and all I could offer him was the stock Hollywood gangster's answer to police grilling – "I don't know nuttin'."

His fuse was short: he blew his top with the ferocity of a pent-up volcano. Whipping me off the chair he threw me face down across the table, grabbed my wrist and for the second time twisted my arm up my back, but with such viciousness I thought he had dislocated my shoulder.

"Tell me about yer pal or I'll bate de livin' daylights out of ye."

With the physique of a bootlace I was a pushover for the Big Fellow. Throwing me about the room was no drain on his physical resources. Unfortunately for him I had one other weakness of which he was unaware: I leaked. I suffered periodically from severe bouts of nose bleeding. My lack of brawn was compensated for by an overabundance

of haemoglobin that occasionally made a break for freedom through one or other of the nostrils of my prominent
snout.

Wracked with pain I was barely conscious of his exhortations to confess to my association with anarchists, revo-
lutionaries and other subversives. On the verge of passing
out I became aware of the familiar warm trickle and
opened my eyes to see the first drops of my life-blood
splatter on the polished wood. The trickle became a deluge
invisible to my persecutor until he jerked me up and
swung me around to face him. The gore splayed out in an
arc across the floor and onto his jacket and shirt. As if it
had suddenly become dislocated his jaw dropped and his
eyes popped out of their sockets as if he had just seen a
ghost.

"What ails ye? I niver laid a hand on ye," he spluttered
as he struggled to regain his composure.

"You banged my face on the table," I lied easily, having
no kinship to George Washington. That he was scared by
the amount of blood that was running from my nose onto
my jacket and to the floor was obvious.

"Sit down dere and hold yer head back," he said, indicating the chair.

He pulled a crumpled handkerchief from his trouser-
pocket and tried to stem the flow. Canute had been more
successful in his confrontation with the tide. The handkerchief was soon sopping and of no further use until
O'Hooligan left the room to rinse it out. He returned carrying the well-rinsed hankie and a damp floorcloth.
Throwing the cool wet handkerchief in my face he turned
and wiped the table clean, got down on his knees and
started to swab the floor.

"Git off home," he babbled, "and don't let me see yer
face agin."

He never had a chance to repeat himself. I was away
like a greyhound out of its trap in pursuit of the hare. I

left him skivvying and babbling incoherently under his breath and rushed out onto the street, purged my lungs of the foul air and gulped avidly the sweet-smelling, free-rolling ozone wafting in from the sea. Moments later, without a word of explanation, Danny was granted his freedom. Before joining me on my way home for my tea he stepped back onto the road to fire a barrage of curses at the building, calling the wrath of God on it and all within.

Big Business

THE PHYSICAL PROCESS of growing up was a painful experience for me. Unlike others of my acquaintance, who grew slowly and imperceptibly, I did my growing like a volcanic mountain – in sudden violent eruptions. Trembling from the effects of some undiagnosed ague I would take to my bed to writhe in agonizing fever for a couple of weeks. It was a regular metamorphosis from which emerged a weaker, thinner and noticeably taller individual than had previously existed. It was a time of great concern for my mother who not only had to nurse me and worry over my prospects of survival but, when I did recover, had to shoulder the financial burden of re-clothing me. Her only compensation was that the clothes I had so quickly outgrown could be washed, pressed and stored away to serve at a future date as hand-me-downs for my younger brother.

The taller and older I grew the more exceedingly embarrassed I became by my long, thin legs. I felt so self-conscious about them that I imagined even the birds laughed as they hopped around on more substantial underpinnings. The pressure I brought to bear on my mother to fix me up with long trousers had been unrelenting, and on that point I had a staunch ally in Danny. He too had long held ambitions in that direction and he was aware that if my mother's resistance could be broken he would have ammunition to fire at home. He was as concerned about the look of his legs as I was of mine, but for a different reason. He looked like he had been born in the saddle, his knees having an antipathy for each other that kept them poles apart. I would have swapped with him any day if limb transplants had been available and had often told him so, but he was not to be consoled.

It was my birthday and when I opened the brown paper parcel that I had found lying on my bed I was over the moon; I had achieved my heart's desire, the best present I could ever wish to get – a pair of long trousers. Within seconds I had discarded what I had long considered to be the hallmark of immaturity and donned the duds of a man. Prancing about, admiring myself in front of the long wardrobe mirror, I thought about Danny and wondered what his reaction would be when he saw me swagger down the street. I had no doubt but that he would be green around the gills and sorely wounded, and I toyed with the idea of rubbing salt into the wound by ignoring him and dismissing him as a mere boy no longer worthy of my companionship.

"You miserable wretch," I assaulted him. "Why didn't you tell me?"

"I didn't know until this morning; anyhow, what about yourself? You kept it dark."

"Somebody has been getting their heads together and kidding us on," I said, dismissing any ideas that it might be coincidence that found us both in long trousers on the same day.

"How do they look from behind?" asked Danny, stepping out before me. "Can you notice my bow legs?"

"No, of course not," I answered. "You just look like you walk with your feet too close together, that's all."

He failed to grasp the sarcasm as we moved on to show the town that this day had given birth to two young men.

"Now that we are in long trousers I think 'tis time we started shaving," remarked Danny, coming to a halt out-

side a chemist's shop and gazing wistfully through the
window.

"What in the hell are you talking about?" I asked, rubbing a hand over my chin. "There's more hair on a goose-
gog than we have between us."

"Never mind about that, we've got to start sometime
and it might as well be now."

"Our first shave?" asked the white-coated proprietor,
who had been busily digging wax from his ears with a car
key. "Ye came to the right place gentlemen. Now let me
see, ah yes, two safety razors and two packets of blades;
now let me see, ah yes of course, two shaving sticks and
two shaving brushes; now let me see, ah yes, two bottles of
after-shave lot. . ."

"Hold it, hold it," interrupted Danny. "We only wanted
two razors and two blades."

"That will never do gentlemen," said the glib-tongued
chemist. "There's more to shaving than scraping your face
with a bit of finely-honed steel: shaving is an art, you
must have the right equipment to do the job properly and,
remember, your skin is delicate and must be treated with
reverence and consideration. Now, where was I? Ah yes,
two bottles of lotion."

"The bastard's cleaned me out," moaned Danny as we
left the shop clutching our two paper bags containing
what we had been assured was the absolute minimum of
essential equipment for a successful first shave.

Danny's kitchen was transformed into a tonsorial par-
lour as we laid out our gear and made preparations for the
shearing. Towel, mirror, basin and boiling water were provided by my host as I stripped to the waist in readiness to
do battle with the facial fuzz. Side by side before the window we competed to whip up the thick, white, foamy
lathers that were soon seeping into ears, mouths and nostrils and cascading down our arms to drip from our elbows
onto shoes and floor. We may as well have worn blindfolds

for what use the mirrors were: the razor-heads vanished from sight in the thick froth that covered our faces like cotton wool masks. Blindly ploughing on with the job I ignored the several nicks I felt as I misjudged the angle of attack. I consoled myself with the thought that I could not do much damage with a safety razor. I had never heard of any man dying of wounds as a consequence of shaving, but when I glanced at Danny I thought I was to be witness to the first such fatality. His face and hands were covered in diluted gore; his lather had turned to a bright pink and rivulets of blood ran down the fingers of his razor hand.

"Stop for God's sake," I shouted. "If you want to kill yourself there are cleaner ways than hacking yourself to death."

His laugh informed me he wasn't suffering, but his accompanying remarks caused me to turn quickly to the mirror.

"Take a gander at yourself," he had said. "Thanks be to Jesus we're not haemophiliacs or we'd be goners," he quipped as we swilled our faces.

Glancing in the mirror I was confronted by the sight of a face that looked as if it had been through the torture of the thousand cuts. Not only had I removed the fine down but in several places I had whipped out the roots.

"Much more of this," I said as I scouted around looking for some cobwebs to stem the flow of blood, "and we'll be needing a skin-graft."

"Ah, it's just like learning to ride a bike," replied Danny. "We'll have to expect a few more scars before we can boast that we have mastered the art of shaving."

Smarting from our wounds and supping some tea we discussed the changes the day had made to our lives and what the effect might be on our life style: we could no longer earn a few bob ploughing through brambles picking blackberries for sale to the co-op; nor could we very well uphold our new-found dignity if we went flogging jamjars to one of the local grocery shops. We concluded that we should have to find other, more appropriate sources of income.

It had been a couple of years or more since the dogs of war had been unleashed to run amok over Europe and most of the world. Thankfully Ireland had so far escaped their depredations, but nevertheless was feeling the pinch in many ways. The world conflict was one of the reasons why blackberry picking had become a lucrative proposition and why jamjars were at a premium. The ever-growing commodity shortages were even hitting the town's blacksmiths, who were being brought to their knees for want of iron and steel, and word had got around that they were prepared to pay any price for supplies, with no questions asked. So it was that Danny and I set ourselves up as part-time scrap-iron merchants.

We began by doing a little market research. We were looking for a smith on whom we could depend to cough up the dough without quibble and who might, when the necessity arose, be prepared to pay a little on account. We found our man in Noonan, a small reedy-looking fellow whom one might expect to be more at home in a haberdashery than wrestling with the hind leg of a horse. Renowned for his skill at the anvil, the demands for his services far exceeded the limitations imposed on him by the acute shortage of malleable metal. He grasped at our proposal like a drowning man might clutch at a straw and confirmed our belief that we had selected the right man, but what really pleased us and clinched the deal was the packet of Woodbines with which he sealed the contract.

For a few weeks we rolled in riches; the town was one big scrapyard to those of us who had eyes to see. I had long before grown tired of hearing my mother tell me that money didn't grow on trees and now here I was picking it up from under my feet. It goes without saying that one couldn't pass an iron bar or part of an old bed-frame over a shop counter as legal tender for a packet of fags, or shove a steel joist through the pay-desk window at the cinema as payment for a seat in the gods. Noonan's smithy was our *bureau de change* where the weight of our wealth was removed from our shoulders and transferred to our pockets.

Life can be as undulatory as the ocean with its crests and troughs and, for the moment, we were riding high. Unfortunately, our acquisitive stroll down Easy Street was soon to be terminated in the congestion caused by chancers jostling and pushing to clamber aboard the gravy-train. Like vultures on discovering a fresh carcass they flocked on the town to pick it clean of its wealth of discarded ferrous metals, and like those feathered scavengers when the bones of the business had been picked dry they moved on in search of other and easier meat.

Danny and I were committed; we had an unwritten contract with Noonan and we intended to fulfill it. Combing the town daily had now become uneconomical, and I considered our best bet lay in moving out to the fields and farms of the very men who were so demanding of Noonan. I put my proposition to Danny.

"Why don't we start cleaning up the countryside?"

"What'ja mean?"

"What I said: clean up the farms and fields. You know there's plenty of scrap out there just going to rust."

"Those bloody farmers wouldn't give you the smell of their breath without being paid for it; you don't expect them to give us iron just for the asking?"

"Who said anything about asking?" I enquired.

"If we didn't ask it would be stealing."

"How do you make that out? Nobody says Robin Hood was a thief. I'm saying we take from the rich to give back to the rich. Is that stealing?"

His hesitation in replying told me I was going to have a few problems with him. I suspected he had been to confession on Saturday and might still be suffering from the hangover. I could think of no greater impediment to lining our pockets than for Danny to be afflicted with an acute case of moral rectitude which, if left untreated, might permanently damage his character.

"What's the bloody matter with you? Why don't you use that grey matter? What use is a five-bar gate lying against a hedge to a farmer who can't get his goods to town because of an un-shod horse? Just think what we could get for one of them."

Whether it was the logic of my argument or the tailpiece, my words penetrated his system like a Cullen's Powder and flushed out the infection.

"I suppose you've got a point. Besides, we could do with the money."

Over the next few weeks we found several gates lying around in semi-retirement and others, crippled and twisted after years of neglect, dumped and forgotten. Steel stakes standing about as redundant fence-posts, flat- and angle-bars that spanned rivers as boundary lines between farms, all mysteriously vanished from the rustic scene, and Noonan rubbed his hands with glee as his stock of raw material grew. Transporting the heavier items presented no problem thanks to the good smith and, unknowingly, his customers. There were always a few donkey-carts lined up outside Noonan's awaiting attention of one sort or another while owners shopped or whiled their time away in a favoured boozer. With a sly wink or a nod of the head Noonan would indicate which vehicle we could avail of to aid our purpose.

We earned a nice steady income right through the winter, but by spring we were roving so far afield that our labours became harder and less rewarding. By March we were pulling in so little dough we were bordering on destitution; if things didn't start to look up we might soon have to stand on street corners, caps in hand, singing for our suppers. Having lived so well for so long it was difficult to adjust to an inadequacy of funds: the bubble had burst and the boom was over. I had no intention of going back to cadging off my mother, not that I had any scruples about accepting hand-outs, but because I knew she couldn't keep me in the style to which I had become accustomed. The business partnership had all but dissolved as we went our own ways, scouting around for another cornucopia that would restore us to solvency.

I stumbled across a new El Dorado in the most unlikely of places – the deserted and dilapidated cottages of a recently vacated slum. Why I should go looking for spondulicks in such an area of deprivation I could never explain, as it looked as promising a prospect as grape-growing in Greenland. I figured that was why I had struck it lucky: who but someone as simple-minded as myself would ever dream of delving into such a desert of desolation? I couldn't have been more elated if I had stumbled on Solomon's mines or Aladdin's cave. I hurried off to find Danny, to let him know we were back in business in a big way.

"There's a fortune here!" he exclaimed as he surveyed the load I had discovered.

"We'd better start moving it straightaway," I suggested. "We don't want to leave it lying around for someone else to find."

"No. It's only two days to Saint Patrick's Day and that would be the best time to start shifting it, when everybody is in town watching the parade."

"I'm not leaving it here that long. What if someone pinches it?" I protested.

"Only an idiot would come down here looking for scrap-iron," came the stinging reply.

"Thanks for the compliment," I retorted.

"Don't mention it."

"Paddy's Day is no good. Noonan will be in town with everybody else and his place will be closed," I reminded him.

"There's tons of iron here; we can't come down in an ass and cart, somebody's bound to spot us, so the best thing is to sneak the bulk of it up to Noonan's house in dribs and drabs when everybody's occupied with the parade."

Reluctantly I had to admit that he was right and agreed to postpone lining my pockets for another couple of days, though it rubbed against the grain.

It was a bitterly cold wind that hurried up and down the street and cut around corners when I met Danny on Patrick's morning. I was well wrapped up in my nice new warm overcoat as added protection against the windy blasts that assaulted me with icy daggers. Danny's only protection was the navy-blue gaberdine mac he had worn so long and so frequently I had come to accept it as his outer skin. Conversation was stifled by the cold as we hurried to the site of our newly-discovered wealth. The iron we had come to rescue from the ravages of rust was in lengths of about three feet and was about half an inch square, convenient dimensions for stacking into neat, compact bundles. The parade wasn't due to start until the afternoon so we devoted the morning to preparation. We had already planned our route to Noonan's house; it would take us along several back streets, across the railway line, along a narrow, usually deserted lane, back across the railway track, through a barbed wire fence, straight into his back yard. What we considered to be a good day's haul was all nicely bundled up and we were sitting smoking when the sounds of "O'Donnell Abú" came riding in on the breeze from the parade in town.

"Come on, let's get moving," said Danny as he chucked away his butt-end and lifted one end of a bundle.

"I'm not carrying that lot in my best coat," I informed him. "I'll get it all mucked up."

"It won't march off on its own unless you're the Sorcerer's Apprentice. Get out your bloody wand or get a hold of it."

"We'll have to wrap 'em up, that's what," I complained.

"Talk sense man, there's nothing around here to wrap 'em in, an' we're wastin' time."

"Yes there is, that thing you call a mac, that's about all it's bloody good for."

He was deeply attached to that piece of gaberdine and it took several minutes of hard and heated argument before I finally convinced him that its days of glory had long gone.

It took about twenty minutes of dodging and weaving to get to Noonan's place and, as we expected, he was out. However, his wife was in and we explained to her the purpose of our visit. She exuded gratitude as she showed us where to deposit our load and prevailed upon us to have some tea and, as we supped, lavished praise on us for foregoing the holiday to provide her husband with the raw material of his trade.

Things went without a hitch until, on our fourth trip, we hit a little snag. To me it was hilarious; I could only sit down and laugh my socks off, but to Danny it was a major catastrophe: he had practically removed the seat of his trousers on a barb of Noonan's wire fence. His sense of humour deserted him and wherever Noonan was holed up his ears should have glowed such was the tirade of abuse Danny hurled on him and his fence. When he had finished cursing the smith into hell he turned his invective on me, accusing me of insensitivity to his plight, causing me to laugh louder and longer. His anger became more intensified as I laughed all the more while he tried vainly to cover his embarrassment.

"How am I going to get home in this state?" He was almost crying. "I can't put that mac on again, it's bloody ruined."

"You're not going home now? We've got work to do."

"If you think I'm going around with the arse out of my trousers you've got another think coming."

"I don't give a damn if you go around in your pelt as

long as we finish the job, we'll never get another chance
like this," I upbraided him. "Look, if it will help you for a
bit, borrow my coat, but bloody look after it."

The offer pacified him and for another hour or more we
scurried back and forth like a couple of ants, piling up the
metal in the smith's yard. It was on what we had planned
to be our last run of the day that Danny came within a
hair's breadth of being beaten to a pulp with one of our
precious bars: he caught the pocket of my new coat on the
same barb that had torn his trousers. All that saved him
from certain death was the picture of the gallows that
flashed across my mind. My coat was ruined; the great L-
shaped tear that gaped at me as I whipped the coat off his
back was enough to cause me apoplexy, but it was the
thought of the hole the repair would make in the day's
profits that caused me the greater anguish. Lashing out
hard-earned dough to some two-bit tailor for an invisible
mending job was a prospect I found hard to stomach.

"You should pay for this," I lambasted him, waving the
coat in front of his face.

"All right, all right, if it will make you happy, but for
God's sake stop griping."

"First thing in the morning then, and don't forget," I
said, calming down a little and changing the subject.
"Let's look for Noonan and tell him what we've got for
him."

"I'm not going down town without an arse to my
trousers. You go and find him, I'll hang on here till you
come back."

It was a hard job finding Noonan but I eventually ran
him down in a back-street bar, almost legless in the ritual
of drowning the shamrock. Taking stock of the state of ine-
briation he was in I congratulated myself for accepting
Danny's choice of Pat's Day for the enterprise: Noonan
was so stupidly intoxicated I could see no reason why we
could not squeeze a few extra quid out of him. I had no lit-

tle difficulty prising him out of his seat and away from his drinking companions, but when the significance of my pleas had seeped through the dense alcoholic fog that clouded his brain I had only one problem left, and that was keeping him on his feet long enough to get him home.

The journey up town was interminable, interspersed with several halts as my sozzled companion regaled me with tales of his prowess at the anvil. I had no interest in what went on in his forge, whether it was shoes or false teeth he made for his customers' horses mattered not a whit to me; all that I was bothered about was getting him back home before he passed out. Right then he was just a drunken money-bag, and I was determined that he would cough up the coinage before conking out.

Danny was still at his post when I got our man through his back gate. Coming in from the glare of the street-lights our hoard of iron looked like a great black mound in the middle of his yard; it could have been a pile of horse manure sitting there in the semi-darkness and as drunk as Noonan was he was not that far gone that he would buy a pig in a poke.

"I can't see what ye've got there," said he. "One of ye go in the house and ask the missus for a torch."

If he had asked for a searchlight it wouldn't have troubled us, we were proud of our day's work and all we wanted was for him to see he had got a good deal, pay us off and let us go on our way. I wasted no time in hurrying to the house and coming back to play a beam of yellow light on our treasure.

"What in the name of Jasus is that!" roared Noonan.

Thinking that his condition had deluded him into thinking he was seeing pink elephants I took it on myself to explain.

"It's the iron we've fetched you."

"Iron? Iron? Ye call that iron? 'Tis rubbish: get it out of here and get it out this very minute."

"Take no notice," I whispered to Danny. "He's stupid drunk."

My whisper hadn't been soft enough or else Noonan had exceptionally sensitive ears.

"Stupid am I? I'll tell ye who's stupid. If ye don't get that rubbish out of my yard this minute I'll call the Guards."

"Nobody's calling you stupid, Mister Noonan," said Danny, "but that's all good iron that we've spent the day carting up here."

"Well ye can cart it back where ye got it from, 'tis all bloody burnt. Where in the hell did ye get it anyhow?"

"From over the fireplaces in those old condemned houses down town," I informed him.

"That explains it. It's been there a bloody hundred years and it's completely oxidized; burnt out and useless. I couldn't get the makings of a nail out of the whole bloody lot. Now clear off and take yer infernal rubbish with ye."

"The ungrateful bastard," I remarked to Danny as I walked close on his heels to protect him from the embarrassment of sniggers and snide remarks about the hole in his trousers.

"Never mind," said he over his shoulder, "but if he expects us to shift that lot again he's in for a surprise. I vote we let him keep it as a Saint Patrick's Day present; after that load of abuse I think he deserves it."

The Missing Link

"AN APPLE A day keeps the doctor away," says the old adage. There may be some truth in it, but it did not cause any doctor I knew to worry unduly about unemployment. They all clocked up their share of overtime tending to our childhood ailments despite the fact that our intake of Adam's favourite fruit far exceeded the number of days in the year. Apples provided us with no protection against the myriads of germs that haunted our street in perpetual search of a good berth, maybe because our total consumption of the inducer of good health was confined to a few weeks every autumn.

Fruit was never acquired by purchase. If any of our gang were to spend money buying apples he would be looked upon as a candidate for incarceration in a nuthouse. There were far more mouth-watering delicacies than fruit to be had. When the odd penny came our way it would immediately develop a homing instinct for Micky Mac's shop. Micky was always waiting behind the counter of the little store, his cherubic face creased in a benign smile of welcome for his penny prodigals as they dragged us through the door. Our reward for their safe return was Micky's gracious invitation to make a selection from the contents of one of the glass jars that crowded his shelves, glittering and sparkling with sweets of infinite variety, the colours of which would put a blush of shame on the face of a rainbow.

When we felt the need for fruit we helped ourselves; that obtained illicitly had a far sweeter taste than any obtained legitimately. Jamsie's celebrated crab-apples were always delicious, but never more so than when he discovered us swarming over his tree like a plague of locusts and tried to swat us with his blackthorn stick. Orchard raiding was no crime in our eyes, even if the law held a different view. Neither was it a sin, and was therefore not worthy of mention in confession. It was a game, a battle of wits between two antagonists – ourselves and the legal owners. It was expected of all lads that they would partake in at least one raid during the season. To some of us it gave an appreciation of autumn as a season of adventure, during which the actual acquisition of fruit was relegated to a position of secondary importance. Nobody who possessed even a lone gooseberry bush was immune from our stealthy forays, but the more difficult and dangerous the orchard the more attractive it became.

On apprehension of a raider some owners were not averse to administering corporal punishment on the spot: a belt in the ear and a toe up the rear. Others, more civilized and enlightened, favoured the heavy hand of the law. Lads unlucky enough to be nabbed considered themselves fortunate to swallow the bitter pill of retribution instantaneously, the aftertaste being of short duration. To be the recipient of a summons meant appearing before the local court, presided over by a man who was the proud owner of one of the finest orchards in the county. He was the victim of many raids carried out by those of us who could be considered to have degenerated into hoodlums of the James Cagney mould. The Justice was renowned as a humorous and just man, but was also reputed to be as merciless as Judge Jeffries when a raider appeared before him. When paying a visit to his place we were aware that being caught could well mean penal servitude for life, or a taste of the cat.

A raiding party usually consisted of from two to four members; the more involved the more likely we would be to betray our presence. Church mice could be suspected of being shod in hob-nail boots when compared to the stealth with which we would approach a target. To our finely tuned ears, as we listened for sound of the enemy, the falling leaves thundered down like hail on a tin roof. When satisfied that we were unlikely to be detected we would break cover and go into the attack, throwing caution to the wind once we had started. Rushing from tree to tree at a fast lick, bags and pockets would be loaded with the biggest and the best. When fully loaded, or at the first sign of danger, we would stampede for the exit, every man for himself and the devil take the hindmost.

As an orchard raider I bore a charmed life; I was never caught. I was no stranger to tight situations and hair's-breadth escapes, but never lost my love of the exhilaration of the incursion or the thrill of the chase. The more successful I was the more audacious I became, until I began to fancy myself as a horticultural Raffles.

My luck was to change and my cocksureness take a knock the day Danny proposed that we go commercial. He had been approached by one of the town's shopkeepers and propositioned with an offer he was too weak-willed to refuse. There was only one reason for this trader's existence and that was an all-consuming drive to accumulate wealth. His shop, though small, contained a plethora of every commodity the local community could desire. Bowing and scraping, fawning over every customer that entered, he gave the impression that any purchase, however small, would be a major contribution to his salvation from utter destitution. To die and leave his wealth behind was his greatest dread, and his preoccupation with finding a method of taking it with him was as much a fixation as was the ancient alchemist's quest for the philosopher's stone. That he would rake a fat profit from what we could supply him we had no doubt, but if he paid us enough for fags and pictures we would be well satisfied.

Danny knew what he termed an "easy mark", a farm run by two brothers and situated about two miles outside town in a locality I had never worked. According to Danny they had plenty on their plates looking after their live-stock and crops and had little or no time to be bothered about their orchard. He assured me that he had visited the place so many times he knew it better than he knew his own backyard. Armed with a couple of sacks and a ball of string we set out on what we hoped would be a fruitful business venture. The reason for the string also called for the wearing of wellies. Danny, not having a pair of his own, had borrowed his father's, which were several sizes too large for him; so large, in fact, that his feet moved two paces before the wellies moved one. At first his movements confused me a little as to whether he was going or staying, but on learning to pace myself to his stop-start motion I accepted it as a minor irritant.

The dense whitethorn hedge that surrounded our Garden of Eden was heavily re-enforced with barbed wire and chicken netting, but had one small gap that Danny had opened up on his first incursion. We crawled through, unconcerned about the brothers whom we credited with having better things to do than standing guard over their apple crop. It took little more than a few minutes to fill both sacks with a fine selection of both "cookers" and "eaters". Stacking both sacks near the opening, we returned to fill our trousers. Stuffing the bottoms well down inside our wellies, we bound them tightly with the string, opened our flies and loaded up. The equivalent of another sack-full, these were destined to be dropped by the roadside and picked up later.

Frankenstein's monster had a more lithesome gait than we as we shuffled our way towards our sacks and the opening. Danny's exclamation when he got down to crawl through the hole shook me to the core.

"Jesus! We're trapped."

Our escape hole was plugged with a roll of barbed wire: the brothers had been aware of our presence and cut off our retreat. Emptying our sacks and undoing our trouser-bottoms, like a pair of scared rabbits we scurried up and down the hedgeside vainly searching for an alternative bolt-hole. The sound of a gate swinging open on its rusty hinges stopped us in our tracks and informed us that we were about to meet our unwelcoming host. Peering beneath the trees we saw we were being approached by a pair of gaitered, corduroy-clad legs, on the lower extremities of which were what appeared to be a pair of size fourteen hob-nail boots.

"Hello there," chirped Danny, "could you tell us the way to town? We seem to have got lost."

"Sure I'll show you the way," boomed a voice as the owner stepped into view.

It was a monster of "Desperate Dan" proportions, wearing a tartan shirt that was struggling valiantly to hold itself together on the enormous body. It had an abnormally large head, surmounted by an unruly mop of jet black hair. The massive jaw was covered in short, black stubble that only a well-honed sickle would be capable of removing. The upper portion of the face was blood-red; either the creature was in an unholy rage or the species to which it belonged had transparent skin. The eyes were hidden from view at the back end of two dark caves that lay beneath a cliff of a brow. By no stretch of the imagination could this gargoyle be classified as of the genus *Homo Sapiens*. Could this actually be the missing link, that elusive creature the scientific world had been seeking for years? Under normal circumstances I would have considered myself privileged to gaze upon such a unique specimen, but right now self-preservation was uppermost on my mind.

111

As if hypnotised, we stood transfixed as it approached and grabbed us by the lugs. Muttering unintelligibly in some strange alien tongue, it dragged us across the orchard, through the gateway and into the farmyard. There were two large mounds of soil in the centre of the yard and what appeared to be a bottomless pit. Releasing our inflamed ears the monster slapped me on the back, flattening me to the ground like a deflated inner-tube. Spitting soil from my mouth and struggling for breath I rolled over on my back to see Danny, arms flailing, suspended by the ankles over the yawning pit.

"This was going to be a well, now it's going to be a grave," bellowed the raging Link. "We've seen ye here many times before, now ye're bringin' up reinforcements. Say yer prayers ye thievin' git."

Danny, struggling to save himself, screamed that he was falling. I could see him begin to slide from his oversize wellies; grabbing the sleeve of his jacket I desperately tried to pull him clear of the hole. The frantic screaming and shouting finally penetrated the great hulk's thick skull and, turning away from the hole, he threw Danny against one of the mounds with a sickening thud.

"Now git out o' here," he roared, aiming a heavy boot at Danny's posterior.

Thanking our stars for getting away so lightly we ran for the gate to the lane only to find ourselves confronted by the other member of the tribe. This chap appeared at first sight to be even more demented than his brother. He was performing some sort of crude ritual dance to the tuneless air of a length of birch that he swung in a whistling arc above his head. His impromptu clog-dance reached its finale on a dull note as my back made contact with his musical instrument in my haste to pass.

Though severely hampered by his wellies, Danny overcame the handicap and raced down the lane like a true thoroughbred, leading the Link by a short head. I was coming up fast on the inside, trying to avoid being crushed on the rails by the birch-wielding brother. As we neared the main road Danny and I were neck-and-neck, spurred on by both boot and birch. It looked as if we were both going to be pipped at the post when divine providence intervened to save us from further suffering. The Link lashed out with a kick that would surely have lifted Danny over the hedge had it connected. Sensing its approach, Danny summoned up enough reserve energy to speed him out of range. The momentum took the Link's foot on an orbital flight-path; as it passed over his head he lost his balance and collapsed on the uneven ground with a howl of agony. My pursuer was reined to a stop by the cries of his stricken brother. Danny and I, with no bonds of kinship or race, felt no desire to offer aid or sympathy, but raced on towards town and safety.

Reaching the shelter of a shop doorway on the outskirts of town, we paused to regain our breath and offer up a silent prayer in gratitude for our deliverance. Suddenly the peace of the quiet street was shattered by the sound of thundering hooves. Peeping cautiously around the edge of the doorway we were amazed to see a pony-and-trap charging down the middle of the street. Stood up in the centre of the trap was the brother; lashing furiously at the foaming steed, he looked for all the world as if he were auditioning for the part of a charioteer in a remake of *Ben Hur*. As it tore past our hiding place we could see the ugly, pain-contorted face of the Link as he bounced up and down on the narrow seat. He was obviously being rushed to the county hospital, though, in his case, we reckoned a vet would have been more appropriate.

"Are you thinking what I'm thinking?" enquired Danny as we watched them go.

"You bet I am," said I, as we turned on our heels and headed back out of town.

The Old Grey Mare

DANNY'S MONEY MAKING schemes aroused little or no
enthusiasm with the lads. There was nothing odd
about that because his schemes invariably
involved much hard graft and little reward. When he came
to me with his latest proposition I was still reeling from
the effects of his previous act of kindness towards me. It
was during the summer holidays when he caught me in
one of my more gullible moments.

"Can you meet me tomorrow morning about half-six?"
he whispered conspiratorially.

"There is something wrong with my ears," I said as I
poked at them with my little finger. I gave a feeble little
laugh and continued, "for a moment there I thought you
said meet you at half-six in the morning."

"That's right, you heard OK. 'Tis money for jam, but
we've got to be there early; it's first come first served, and
half the town will be there."

"What's this marvellous job that everybody wants?"

"Look, you want it or you don't? If you don't I'll get
somebody who does."

If there was some easy money going I wasn't going to
hand it on a plate to someone else, so I promised to meet
him at half-six.

When I arrived at the appointed meeting place there
was no sign of Danny, and though I wasn't very surprised
at that I felt a little put out. Pacing back and forth to keep

warm I noticed a gang of tough-looking men loitering against the wall about fifty yards away. Making a mental note not to allow myself to get any closer to them I was unaware of Danny sloping up behind me; he didn't stop, but ambled on towards the suspected cut-throats, beckoning me to follow.

"Hurry up," he shouted as a cattle truck trundled up the road and pulled in beside the shifty looking group. It had hardly stopped when they started scrambling up the rails and over the top.

"Jump on quick," said Danny, "he'll be away as soon as he's full."

"What the hell's going on Danny?" I asked when we were wedged safely aboard. "Where are we going?"

"We're going to the bog," he said, delaying his reply until the truck had moved off.

"To the bloody bog!" I yelled. "I'm not going to any bloody bog."

"'Tis too late now. Anyway you'll like this bog, 'tis all done by machine."

"What bog? And if it's all done by machine what do they want us for?"

"'Tis at the other side of the Stacks, and we've got to keep the machines going."

"I'm no engineer, and these fellows don't look like engineers either," I said, casting an eye over our travelling companions.

"Well," he drawled, "'tisn't exactly engineering, but you'll see when we get there."

It had been close to seven when we left town and it showed quarter to seven by the office clock when we went to present ourselves.

"The clock's slow," I remarked to Danny as we took our turn in the queue.

"'Tis not," said Danny.

"We left town just before seven, we've been on the road

nearly an hour, and that clock says quarter to seven so it must be bloody slow."

"That's country time," came the reply.

"What in the hell is country time," I enquired, though I had heard mention of it a few times before.

"They don't alter the clocks like they do in town," he informed me.

"What time do we start?" I asked.

"Eight o'clock."

"Town or country time?"

"Country time."

"If we start at eight o'clock country time, what are we doing here at eight o'clock town time?"

"It's about an hour's walk to the job," came the nonchalant reply.

"A bloody hour's walk? And what time do we finish?"

"Six o'clock."

"Country time?"

"No, town time."

"So, if we finish work at six, town time, we'll be back down here at six o'clock country time, which means we won't be home till eight o'clock town time. That's a bloody long day, if you ask me."

"I suppose it is if you look at it that way," replied Danny uneasily.

"Look at it any way you like, it's still a long day."

"Well, the money's good," he said, as if that were some consolation.

I was soon to find out how good the money was. There was a bit of a squabble going on at the desk between the clerk we were waiting to see and two of the men who had travelled out from town with us. From what we could hear they had earned too much money the week before and were being transferred to different jobs. The clerk cared nothing for production, all that bothered him was that no mere manual worker should earn more than he did. They either changed jobs or went on day-rate, take it or leave it. They took it and walked out muttering profanities under their breaths.

"Haven't seen you here before, have you brought your cards?"

Thinking he wanted a friendly game of brag or something, I said, "No, but I'll fetch a pack tomorrow."

He gave me a peculiar look, opened his mouth to speak, but seemed to find himself a little lost for words. Rather excitedly Danny stuck his head over my shoulder to exclaim, "They won't be ready till Friday, sir". That seemed to satisfy the man and he quickly regained his power of speech.

"Oh, very well, but seeing as it's your first day here you had better go with the girls; and you go with him," he said, turning to Danny. "And don't forget, I want both your cards here before next week."

"It was your insurance cards he wanted, you ass," said Danny as we stepped out the door.

"How was I to know that? Anyway the work can't be too hard if we're working with girls. I've changed my mind about the place; I think I'm going to like it."

"I told you that you would, didn't I? Here are the girls now," he nodded with his head.

Looking in the direction of his nod I was struck dumb. Each and every one was an Amazon of elephantine proportions. If there was one who had less flesh on one limb than I had on my entire body I failed to see her. The ground trembled as they thundered by, laughing and joking like carefree children going on a picnic. They were all attired in similar fashion, blue bonnets, blue or black knee-length dresses and newly washed and ironed pinafores. They were all shod in wellingtons, though whether these were full length or cut-down it was hard to tell as the tops were hidden from view in overhanging folds of loose flesh.

"Come on, let's get going or we'll lose them," said Danny,

shaking me out of shock.

"Holy Mother of God, will I ever learn?" I asked myself as I followed him up the rutted track.

Maybe if I had paid more attention to my English teacher I would not have been so disillusioned as I was when I had my first encounter with "mechanization". I had come here innocently believing that the most laborious task I would be called on to perform would be the administration of a few drops of lubricant every now and then to the mechanical marvel's grating joints. The contraption that I had expected to do all the hard graft was nothing more than a mobile conveyor belt high-tailing it down the bog, closely followed by the girls, arms moving like high-speed flails desperately trying to satisfy its appetite for the dried sods of turf that had been laid out in neat rows by the cutting and spreading machine that had passed over the same section of bog several days before. Gorging and disgorging in its crab-wise cross-country canter, the brainchild of modern technology was too nimble for its ministering handmaidens.

This was why Danny and I came to have a soft number; not soft in the cushy sense, but soft underfoot. It was all right for Danny who like everybody else in sight was shod in wellington boots, but I wore nothing more substantial than a pair of light shoes designed for use on nothing rougher than a well-paved walkway. Handed two wicker baskets by the man in charge, we were ordered to collect and fetch to the headland all the sods of turf the hard-pressed maidens had missed. Lightweight that I was I had no problems to begin with. It was when I had filled my basket and attempted to lift it that I found myself in trouble. I had sunk ankle-deep in the mire, and the more determined I was to free myself the deeper I went. Abandoning my basket I used both hands to withdraw my feet from the clutching goo, leaving embedded in the murky depths my one and only pair of shoes.

118

Consoling myself with the thought that things couldn't get worse, I fished them out, cursing Danny and all his ancestors into eternity. I was on a hiding to nothing, and I knew it, as I struggled to make a few bob. I spent more time and wasted more energy digging myself out of the mire than I did moving turf. By lunch-time I was all-in and saw no hope of my surviving much longer in either town or country time. Damp as my spirits were they were to become even damper: it started to rain. Like everything else out here, even the word "rain" had a different meaning to anything I had ever known. It didn't fall down in drops from an overhead cloud; it flowed over us like a river. Sweeping across the bog-land in a fine, dense drizzle, it had everything and everybody saturated within moments, and there was no shelter.

Outside the frozen wastes of the Polar regions or the burning sands of the desert, there must be few places on the planet where there is no shelter whatever from the elements, yet I had found one right here in Ireland. Everybody else had come prepared, waterproof clothing appeared as if by magic, while my entrepreneurial friend and I lay saturated behind a few sods of turf. If the rain had saved me from premature death from exhaustion, it would certainly cause me to expire through exposure or drowning. Building a ramshackle shelter with sodden sods, we huddled together, drawing comfort from each other's misery, Danny at least having his ears warmed by the tirade of abuse I heaped on him.

It was an hour or more before the foreman came by in his oilskins to inform us that work had ceased for that day. As he commiserated with me on my unfortunate introduction to modernized bog-work, I couldn't find the heart to tell him what I wished he would do with it. The journey down to the office was a nightmare; whipped along by a rising wind the driving rain lashed my half-frozen body with a ferocity that caused me to think it might penetrate my skin and dilute my blood. On reaching the office, those of us who were awaiting the cattle-truck crowded in for shelter while the local workers scattered for their nearby homes. The under-worked clerk resented the situation, but thought it wise to keep his mouth shut and get on with the pretence of working. I stripped off all but my trousers and, unknown to the clerk, borrowed his towel from its nail by the fire and rubbed myself down, bringing some warmth back to my body.

The truck driver didn't depend on transporting idiots for a living and was probably spending the day carting other, more sensible creatures like cattle or sheep about. His contract was to dump us in the morning and pick us up in the evening and it meant nothing to him that we were rained off; we would just have to wait until it was six o'clock. It was a long afternoon. My trousers had almost dried out as they clung to my legs, my shoes were sodden and cold to the feet while my other clothes hung from my fist in a crumpled wet ball. But with every tick of the wall-clock my spirits revived, and through the steamed-up window could be seen a break in the clouds. Dead on the dot of six country time the truck's arrival coincided with the departure of the last of the rain.

There is life after death. I know: my day in the bog proved it. My relationship with Danny suffered a slight setback, but soon recovered. The only thing that really narked me was that I never got paid for my few hours' labour. Maybe someday I shall pluck up courage to call out there or write and ask for it. After all these years, with interest it should be worth a pretty penny.

Now, here I was again, lending an ear to another of his madcap schemes. My experience and better judgement told me to run away from him, but my greed got the better of me. We were sharing the same desk and every time the teacher turned his back Danny threw another tempting tit-bit my way. We were wasting our time sat here, according to him. We would be better occupied out and about making a few bob. He knew where a couple of good lads were required for a few days work, cash in hand, no questions asked. Even if the work was hard, which it wasn't, it would be a damn sight better than having to tolerate the frequent thrashings from the black-frocked flagellator who was supposed to be responsible for our education. He was referring to the man we had dubbed "the Very Christian Brother," an exceedingly devout man who believed that humanity should pay the price for sin. I couldn't say I had any quarrel with his beliefs, after all I never objected to the odd Hail Mary as retribution for my own transgressions, but what I did object to was being a surrogate penitent, especially when it meant suffering physical violence. Whether proxy penance cut any ice with Himself or not I never figured out, but the Very Christian Brother was a confirmed devotee of the practice and wielded the leather strap more frequently than he did the chalk.

It was all too much for Danny. He was going to take a few days off and take life easy doing a bit of work. With his hand over his mouth, and in hushed tones, he filled me in with all the gen. Starting on Monday the road by his house was to be dressed with loose chippings, and anybody with a horse and cart and a willingness to work could be set on. He had a cart in his yard and knew where he could borrow a horse. Why didn't I join him? My experience with the bog was still fresh in my mind and made me very reluctant to accept the offer, but my hesitation was short-lived when I was awarded the honour of being elected the penitent of the day. If I were going to have welts on the palms of my hands it was preferable that they come from the handle of a shovel than from the business end of a viciously-wielded length of leather.

Danny had just completed harnessing the horse when I arrived in his yard. It was a mare, a grey mare, and not the colour that was inherent in her genes but the grey bestowed upon the venerable by Mother Nature. She was also afflicted with the most severe case of spinal curvature that I had ever clapped an eye on. Its gravity was such that she almost had five-point contact with the ground. Knock-kneed and fleshless, with head bowed and eyelids drooping, she looked like a reject from a knacker's yard.

"Who helped you to carry her here?" I asked sarcastically.

"What do you mean? There's bags of life in her, I can tell you."

"We'd better get moving then; by the sound of it it's escaping out her arse."

"Stop bloody moaning and help me get her hitched for God's sake," he barked.

"Come on Dolly old girl, let's get you hitched up," he cajoled, but deafness seemed to be another of her geriatric infirmities, he getting no response.

"Why not try a carrot?" I asked hopefully.

"A brilliant idea, and seeing as we're trying to back her up which bloody end do you suggest we offer it to?"

"Don't lose your wool, I was only trying to help," I said, feeling a little hurt.

"Well if you want to help grab one of those shafts, we'll have to take the cart to her," he replied, calming down a little.

The trauma of the harnessing had been disturbing enough for old Dolly, but to be hitched to a cart again was more than she was prepared to accept. For the next five minutes the three of us performed what might be described as a ritual hitching dance; Danny and I with the shafts cradled in our arms hopping in one direction, with Dolly side-stepping in another. Like an equine Carmen Miranda she gave a dazzling performance of the rumba as she dodged and weaved to avoid being snared between the shafts. In exasperation Danny left me to support the shafts while he charged at Dolly's gyrating buttocks. The

shock of the onslaught halted her rave-up long enough for
me to pull the cart forward and entrap her. Before she
realised what had hit her she was hitched, and we were
ready for the road.

We were a long time getting there. Each of Dolly's steps
was followed by a short pause, as if she had difficulty in
remembering the sequence of movements involved in locomotion. The early morning atmosphere was tinged with a
blue haze as Danny heaped profanities upon her drooping
head.

"God blast you Dolly you'll do this job if it kills me," he
yelled, his face scarlet with rage and frustration, while
laying in to her rump with his shovel.

Slow as our progress was we were first on site. Piles of
stone chippings had been dumped along the roadside; our
job would be to load the cart and, as Dolly ambled her way
forward, to follow behind lightening her load with our
shovels as we spread the contents of the cart over the surface of the road.

The first pile of chippings was situated only yards from
Danny's gate and we set to work with the enthusiasm of
the new starter wishing to impress. We had the cart half
loaded when the first of our fellow-workers arrived with
his cart and spirited young roan, and by the time the
ganger-man showed up we were ready to move off. A smile
of approval lit the man's face on seeing the two willing
younglads who looked like making short shrift of the task
ahead. Listening attentively as he explained his require-
ments and issued instructions, we were taken by complete
surprise when a groan escaped from Dolly's lips as she collapsed in a limp heap between the shafts.

"My God, she's dropped dead," I gasped.

"Dropped dead my arse," said Danny, "she's dropped
asleep, the lazy bastard."

That he was right was evidenced by the snoring sounds
that began to emerge from her twitching nostrils. The load

had slipped forward on the cart and was spilling over her nether ends, partially burying her. Danny wasted no time in bringing his shovel back into play to whip the sleep out of her and get her into a position where she could be unhitched and put back on her feet. The look on the face of the ganger was one of incredulity, while wry smiles creased the faces of the others who stood around.

It was another long and desperate struggle to re-hitch and get re-loaded. Our fellow-workers had depleted the pile and moved on, leaving only the ganger to stay and watch the pantomime that was having an impromptu performance on the open road. Danny had Dolly by the head, I slapped her rump in encouragement, and she took her first and only step forward. Her hoof came firmly down on Danny's right foot, and remained there. It was Dolly's trump card and she played it well; she had him where she wanted him. Oblivious to the profanities and abuse heaped upon her, she just blinked sleepily as the colour drained from Danny's pain-wracked face. In desperation he bent down, encircled her leg with his arms, and vainly attempted to remove the offending hoof. The ganger-man and I rushed to his assistance and after a struggle managed to release him. He hopped across to the hedge, threw himself down and cradled his injured foot in both hands. He considered it insult added to injury when the ganger-man suggested that we call it a day and go home. Between cursing old Dolly and groaning in pain he pleaded for another chance, but the ganger-man was adamant; the old girl was past it and should be taken back to wherever she belonged and allowed to live out her retirement in peace and tranquillity.

When Danny recovered from his ordeal, we off-loaded the chippings, unhitched Dolly and pushed the cart to the side of the road. Turning the old girl towards home we witnessed a miraculous change in her demeanour: her step lightened and her pace quickened, the sleepiness vanished from her eyes and I fancied I noticed a twinkle that told me she knew she had won. We turned her loose in her field, where she immediately broke into a canter and on reaching the far side kicked her hind legs in the air in what could only be interpreted as a gesture of derision. We returned for the cart and one to each shaft began the laborious task of drawing it back to Danny's yard. We trudged despondently towards the gate, our progress impeded by the loose chippings that cracked and grumbled beneath the wheels.

"Another fine mess you've gotten us into, Stanley," I quipped.

"Shut your stupid gob," came the sharp retort.

Before we turned off the road I caught a glimpse of the ganger-man, who was stood on the other side. He appeared to be in joyous mood as he sang softly to himself. The tune had a familiar ring, and raising his voice the words stung as they followed us up the drive.

"The old grey mare, oh she ain't what she used to be."

A Victim of
Circumstance

THE RESPONSE TO the soft plaintive call of the
Angelus bell was not supplication and prayer but
the daily stampede of the wage-slaves as they bolted from factory, shop and office at the end of another battle in the eternal struggle for survival. It was the signal
for the town to down tools, throw off its working clothes
and turn its back on striving. What was left of the day was
a man's own, he was no longer in hock to the big-bellied
master but free to do with his time exactly what he wished
within reason and the confines of his financial limitations.
From the domestic bliss of an evening by the fireside with
book or radio to the more strenuous exertions of "cutting a
rug" at a local dance-hall, options were diverse and dis-
parate. Entertainment opportunities were sufficient to satisfy all tastes, except perhaps for those whose idea of a
night out was a Saturnalian orgy – the civic fathers never
did get around to the provision of flesh-pots or sin-bins as
part of the social services.

The staid and settled older generation might settle for
an evening walk out of town and around the country lanes,
staunch advocates of the exercise as a stimulating and
therapeutic form of relaxation. For the young and impecunious bucks and fillies walking was confined to the main
street promenade. The days of the Kerry dancing when the
lads and lassies met and frolicked on the platforms outside
town had long gone, supplanted by corrugated-iron cov-

ered monstrosities masquerading as dance-halls. Without
the spondulicks to gain admission to these hops the promenade filled a void. It gave to the girls an opportunity to
display their blossoming charms, to court coyly the admiring glances of brilliantined Lotharios and with luck perhaps acquire an evening beau. For the boys it was a stage
on which to strut up and down like predacious peacocks in
search of a conquest that might lead to little more than a
kiss and a cuddle in a darkened doorway, but feed fuel to
boasts of their prowess as Casanovas. It was a harmless if
not salubrious evening ritual symbolic of an era of innocu-
ousness and innocence.

Proliferating in groups on every street corner and as living
buttresses outside the town's more important buildings
were the corner boys who, had they lived in old Jericho,
might very well have altered the course of history.
Denigrated and scorned as work-shy layabouts, they took
their simple pleasures from discourse and conversation.
Here in these little groups were congregated men of
unrecognised genius. Military tacticians beside whom the
world's greatest generals were mere schoolboys incapable
of commanding a regiment of toy soldiers, and theologians
who made the pronouncements of the pope sound like the
babblings of an altar-boy. Pontificating and propounding,
they whittled their evenings away righting the world's
wrongs, proposing ingenious remedies for the nation's ills,
and hatching foolproof schemes for the pauperization of
the town's bookmakers.

Though each group was autonomous they had close
associations with every other group through a signal system which was completely unintelligible to outsiders, but
as efficient at transmitting news and gossip as smoke-sig-
nals or tom-toms. It was a service that was of great benefit
to another nighthawk who could be found lounging around
the streets on a late evening, a solitary sentinel whose
presence was not a quest for pleasure but rather the visi-

ble symbol of the forbidden fruits that were to be availed of behind the closed doors and darkened windows of the town's speakeasies. Right up to ten o'clock these establishments operated legitimately as pubs where any man could stop off to slake a thirst, or, if one was so inclined and had the dough, could become stupidly inebriated. After ten the doors were officially closed to all except the bona fide traveller, a title which in those days was applied to anyone who had strayed more than three miles from home.

For some strange, inexplicable reason, men who could walk past a hundred legally open pubs as if they were total abstainers would, after the doors had closed, develop an overwhelming desire for alcohol. The phenomenon would occur in homes all over town when clocks struck the magic hour of ten. Otherwise decent, law-abiding citizens would rise from their comfortable armchairs or sofas, don hat and coat, abandon wives and children and skulk through the streets, furtively tapping on pub doors and windows in a desperate search for booze. Though some of the strait-laced might despise and condemn publicans as home-wreckers and purveyors of poisons, there were many among the profession who had hearts of gold. While it meant contravention of the law and danger to their pockets, these good men could not, and would not, sit idly by ignoring the plaintive pleas of a nightly thirsty horde. In furtherance of what they considered a necessary public service, albeit an illegal one, they instituted the profession of "look-out man".

The qualifications required for the post were two: a sharp eye and a thick skin. Short-sightedness was of little use to a man who was expected to discern the dark-blue uniform of the cop hiding in the shadows at the other end of town, or to recognise the off-duty man among the crowds milling home from the pictures. A thick skin coupled with a hard heart was of almost equal importance. To be able to turn a deaf ear to the heart-rending pleas of an undesirable, and then suffer the abuse dished out as he staggered off to the next watering hole, took courage and strength of character. The job, like any other, had its compensations as well as its drawbacks. The odd tip from a grateful customer and the pint left behind the bar were welcome bonuses, but to have to stick to one's post on a windy, rain-lashed street, hearing the laughter and song wafting from the interior of a warm and cosy den, was a test of stamina and dedication.

Some of the men employed in this essential service had been around so long they had become part of the street furniture and were known to all, including the men in blue. Even these guardians of the law were not immune from the after-hours malady and were never reluctant to avail of the service when opportunity presented itself. Unspoken agreements were entered into, in which, whether on duty or off they could slip in for a quick draught on the house in return for temporary blindness and loss of hearing. However, nothing in this world is perfect; to err is human; but when the errant one is a copper forgiveness comes only from the divinity, as one unfortunate cop I knew learned to his cost.

The evening was humid, the pavements were hot to the flat feet that had been pounding the late evening shift. Sidling up to the look-out at his favourite pub, he opened his mouth to reveal a parched tongue, the "open sesame" to the delights of a free drink. Refreshed and satisfied he wiped the froth from his lips, tapped on the inside of the door to be let out, and resumed his beat. He strode leisurely down the street, rounded the corner and came face to face with his Duty Sergeant.

"I think it's time we paid Mulligan's a visit," said the Sergeant without stopping.

Following closely behind his superior he wondered if the look-out would have the sense to size up the situation and give the signal to clear the house. But the look-out, who only a few moments before had bade the Guard goodnight, had no suspicion of treachery as he watched them approach. On the contrary: thinking the Sergeant was being brought along for a sly refresher he unlocked the door and with a smile and a friendly word invited them in. With notebooks out and pencils poised they elbowed their way around the crowded bar taking names and addresses from customers who would not be in the least surprised to see a cop use strong-arm tactics to arrest his own grandmother, but to whom this double-cross plumbed the depths of despicability.

I had no ambitions to become a look-out man for a lawbreaking publican, as a matter of fact I had no ambitions to become anything; I was quite content to take life as it came, to stumble along from one day into another. As long as I had a few bob to see me through the day I saw no need to worry about the morrow, but, like any other normal lad, when the auspicious moment arrived it was welcomed with open arms.

It was Friday night, the pictures were over and with a few pals I was doing a last round of the town before retiring to home and bed. Late though the hour was the street was fairly crowded with promenaders, corner-boys, late night revellers and the usual sprinkling of look-out men. One of the latter, whom I knew fairly well, grabbed me by the elbow as I passed, pulled me close and whispered confidentially:

"Would you like a nice little job?"

"What doing?" I asked in surprise.

"This job: looking after a boozer."

"Not likely, I'm not holding a wall up all night; I've better things to do," I snapped.

"No 'tis not nights, 'tis Sundays," he said. "Murphy's want a man for Sundays; finish about seven, dead cushy."

I could do with a few extra bob, and if it didn't interfere with my social life I was prepared to consider it.

"How much does it pay?" I enquired.

"A pound for the day; a pound and your grub," he answered.

A quid and my grub for standing around doing nothing? He was talking my language now.

"All right then, I'll give it a try," I told him. "I'll give it one day at least to see how it goes."

"Now you're talking. Go up in the morning and tell them I sent you; you'll be all right."

The following morning I presented myself to the widow Murphy as she stood behind the bar. With clothes brushed, hair combed and shoes shining I stood confidently gazing over the counter at her pleasant, smiling face.

"I'm here," I said.

"I can see that," said the widow, "and who might you be?"

"I'm your new look-out man," I replied.

"Oh, you are, are you; and who told you that?"

"Mick, he told me you were in need of a good lad."

"There are more Jack Barrys than one, what Mick sent you?" she asked impatiently.

"O'Brien's Mick, I was talking to him last night." My confidence was on the ebb.

"Well, if he sent you, you must be all right," she smiled. "Do you know what the job entails? Do you know all the Guards?"

"I know every Guard in town and I could spot them a mile off." I reeled off the names and descriptions of every cop that might be a nuisance to her illicit trade, and succeeded in convincing her that she would have nothing to worry about with me on guard outside her door.

"A pound a day and your food. Be here at ten in the morning; we'll see how you go."

I tapped nervously on the door at the stroke of ten. The barmaid opened up and after I explained who I was she ushered me into the kitchen where a corpulent, jolly-looking cook invited me to sit down and have breakfast. I neglected to tell her that I had already dined but as a growing lad I felt that a second helping of bacon and egg would do me no harm. Congratulating myself on having fallen on my feet, I sat back to enjoy my second mug of tea when the widow arrived to tell me it was time I started earning my money. Handing me the key to the bar door she instructed me on the system of signals I was to use to warn of danger, and bundled me out onto the pavement to make good my promises and prove my worth.

I was alone. If I had been stranded on a desert island I could not have been more alone. There were people abroad on the street but I was no longer one of them: I was just a pair of eyes. I felt that I had prostituted myself; flogged myself to the widow for a quid. My self-esteem was taking a hammering. I felt like going back in and telling the widow to find herself another boy. While I was trying to pluck up the courage to take the coward's way out and jack it in my first customer arrived to beg for admission. He didn't know it but he made me feel good; his craving for a drink transformed me from a self-deprecating dogs-body to a vainglorious autocrat. I alone had the power to grant or refuse his request, and I intended to make good use of my authority.

"Ask me nicely," I commanded.

"Please sir, I just want one pint, that's all I want sir," he pleaded.

So it was "sir" now; much better, but not good enough for my liking.

"I don't know; I'll think about it," I teased.

"Please don't be like that sir. One drink sir, I'll be no bother," he clutched my sleeve and begged. It was getting better, soon I would have him on his knees and kissing my hand as if I were the bishop.

"All right then," I relented a little. "Only one, mind, and next time be more respectful."

I turned the key in the lock and bade him enter.

"God bless you, God bless you sir, you're a gentleman," he croaked as he slipped inside.

I had hardly removed the key when the door was torn open with such force it was nearly whipped off its hinges and the quare fella came flying through to land on his rump in the middle of the pavement.

"What did you let him in for?" roared the angry widow. "He's the biggest latchico in town. If you want to keep your job keep him out."

This was a good start: my first salaried job and I was making a hames of it. I resolved to be more careful in future and not let anyone in that I could not personally vouch for. No more bums would pass through these portals. Unfortunately for my employer's regulars I knew none of them and, refusing to listen to their pleas and entreaties, I told them to take their hook elsewhere.

"What in the name of God do you mean by turning my customers away?" yelled the widow as she came charging out. "Do you want to drive me out of business?"

"I don't want to let any undesirables in," I answered in defence.

"You certainly won't if you let nobody in! Just open the door to whoever wants a drink, I'll tell you as we go on who I don't want back. It's getting on for eleven and we haven't sold a drop yet."

Taking her advice I quickly got the hang of it and business was soon booming; what was more, I had not seen a uniform since I'd started. This was really easy money; I only regretted that I had not fetched along a book or magazine to while away the time.

"It's Casey and O'Donnell," the voice said.

I looked up to see a young chap astride a bike by the kerb.

"What are you talking about?" I asked.

"Casey and O'Donnell, they're the two on pub-duty

today. I've just seen them coming out of Mass; they've gone up Rock Street so you should be all right for a while."

"What do you mean by pub-duty men? All I need to see is the uniform, I don't bloody care who's in it."

"Hasn't anyone told you? 'Tis plain-clothes men on Sunday."

What sort of trickery was this? I had expected a straight game and now I was being told that my opponents were dealing from the bottom of the pack.

"Don't worry, you'll recognise them all right," my informant continued, "they're both wearing macs and trilbys; you can't mistake them."

I thanked him for his information as he rode off to inform the next look-out. I paused for a moment to reflect on the deviousness and cloven-hooved behaviour to which some people were prepared to stoop to prevent honest men earning a few pennies. Such perfidiousness was not going to intimidate me; I knew these two and had no doubt that I would be able to recognise them a mile off, and beat them at their contemptible game.

I was aware that my most trying moments would come during the exodus from last Mass. Why this service should be so well attended always baffled me. It could be the most long-drawn-out and boring Mass of the week, depending on which priest delivered the sermon. There were one or two priests who could make a quote from the bible sound as long-winded and incomprehensible as a major work of Bill Shakespeare. These fellows always did their thing at twelve o'clock Mass so I avoided it like the plague; nevertheless, it was the best-attended Mass of the day. The logorrhoea was excellent therapy for insomniacs, but for the majority it was the penalty for late nights and late rising; before the last blessing they were bounding out onto the street as if the devil himself were after them.

When I saw the first wave swirling up the street I felt like turning and running for my life. Although I knew my

134

foes I couldn't see myself picking them out among this lot! Wavering in indecision it was quickly brought home to me that I was a born pessimist, too hasty at underestimating my abilities. Maybe it was more luck than acumen that caused me to turn my attention away from the tide of home-going worshippers and cast my eye in the opposite direction. It wasn't a moment too soon and almost seconds too late: my two jokers were just emerging onto the street from a side lane when I turned my head. I tapped out my warning on the glass and edged myself a few paces to the window of the next-door premises where I wrapped myself in an air of nonchalance. The frontage against which I had re-positioned my person was also that of a public house, but one which never indulged in illicit trade, a matter of common knowledge to everyone in town. The proprietor, a law-abiding pillar of rectitude, was a man of independent means to whom the business was only a pastime. Living alone he was his own man, allowing himself only two luxuries in life: a cigarette and a long lie-in. During the week his door opened several hours after the streets had aired, and on Sundays not at all.

Whether my lounging against his window aroused suspicions in the two cops or not I do not know, but they by-passed the widow's to stop and bang hell out of his door. I thought it advisable to make myself scarce and crossed the road to lose myself among the crowd that had stopped to gape. The delay in opening must have further fuelled the suspicions of the two door-thumpers because their banging became louder and more impatient, and attracted even more gawpers. Like flies to a fresh cowpat the multitude grew, choking the street and creating a traffic jam. Drivers and their passengers abandoned cars to crowd up closer for a better view of the show. De Valera would have done well to have attracted as big a gathering to one of his rallies.

I only caught a momentary glimpse of the publican's

face when he opened his door to allow the two boys to push in. It bore the stamp of amazement; eyes and mouth were of equal aperture, while a newly-lit cigarette dangled precariously from his lower lip. That he could be suspected of illicit trade was bad enough, but to be actually raided was an affront to his integrity and a slur on his character that he never would forgive. Before closing the door he turned to glance at the crowd of rubbernecks and his appearance confirmed his expression of innocence. Crumpled pyjamas, tatty dressing-gown and ill-fitting carpet slippers were not the attire one would expect of a man entertaining customers. The heart of the crowd went out to him, and he displayed his appreciation by saluting us with a weak smile before closing the door in our sympathetic faces.

Some of the crowd dispersed with the closure of the door, but many remained to boo and cat-call at the two disappointed cops when they would re-emerge after their fruitless search of the premises. Dreams of bogy-baiting were shattered when the door did open to reveal a shame-faced imbiber who, with head hung low, elbowed his way through and vanished in the crowd. The look on the face of the publican when he first opened up was nothing compared to that which showed on the faces of the waiting spectators. To learn that the pope had turned Protestant wouldn't have been a greater surprise than this. Here was a man whom everybody looked upon as a paragon of propriety, a man who had frequently boasted that he would never sell a drink outside permitted hours and who was loud in his condemnation of those that did, caught red-handed in his transgression. To the town gossips this was manna from heaven: the man's reputation was in shreds.

As the door opened again and again to reveal even more publicity-shy boozers who scurried away like cockroaches from the light, the incredulous onlookers turned to each other seeking confirmation that their eyes were not deceiving them. I heard someone ask how such a little bar could accommodate so many. I could have offered an answer of sorts if it were not for the fact that I was speechless: every man that came out of this pub had only a short while before been ushered by me into the widow's.

I was not to find out until later, when all the hubbub had died down, what had actually transpired. My warning taps on the window had sounded so urgent that the widow had deemed it wise to clear the house. Every one of her customers was shown the back door and told to take his drink with him. Taking precautions one step further they slipped over the wall into the yard of what was considered to be the safest house in town.

Life can be full of surprises, and what could be more surprising for a law-abiding publican than to have the law descend on him on a peaceful Sunday morning, and to discover at that inopportune moment that he was inadvertently harbouring in his backyard thirty slightly inebriated revellers with glasses in hand? The shock, the ignominy and, of course, the fine left a deep scar, changing the poor man's life style completely. For me, the least surprising aspect of the whole affair came a couple of weeks later when he sidled up to me at my post outside the widow's door and asked me where he might find himself a good look-out man, mumbling something like, "If a man has the name he might as well join in the game."

New Shoes

I T WAS A long time since I had made my confession and
I was surprised to find that my confessor suffered
from the same problem.

"They don't look the same any more," I had said.

"How do you mean?" he enquired.

"Well, they're not skinny little things any more, running
around with one knicker-leg hanging lower than the other.
They've filled out and look quite, well, you know . . ."

"I know what you mean; I've noticed it myself," he
answered.

"I wonder what it would be like to kiss and cuddle one,
just like they do in the pictures?"

"There's only one way to find out," said Danny. "Let's go
down town tonight and try to pick a couple up."

Sex had entered our lives: we were no longer children.
Many moons had passed since we had abandoned childish
things, but this was the first time that we had openly
admitted to each other that girls held a fascination and
that we were ready and willing to embark on ventures of a
sexual nature.

We soon learned that if we were to have any success in
this field we should have to develop techniques entirely
different from those we employed to acquire the other
pleasures of life. We discovered that girls were individuals
who could be very selective about whom they allowed to
play court. We were hopelessly lost in our first attempts at

wooing and suffered repeated repulses. Our self-confidence took a battering, and when we were openly laughed at for our efforts we seriously discussed the attractions of a monastic life.

It didn't help or boost the ego to slink into the shadows of some shop doorway and see a lad, whom we considered to be our inferior in looks, physique or intelligence, stride by with some glamour-puss dangling from his arm and gazing into his eyes as if he were Adonis reincarnated. There was some secret formula in the art of courtship which eluded us; a magic key to unlock the female heart. All enquiries drew a blank as those whom we knew to have it were evasive in their answers, pretending they knew of no such open sesame.

Our luck changed when Sean arrived in town. We met him on his first evening stroll down the main street; we didn't need to ask where he had come from, he had "bog-man" written all over him. He looked like a fish out of water when we first noticed him passing on the other side of the street, and when he returned again on our side of the road we couldn't but feel some sympathy for him. We hailed him as he passed and struck up a conversation. He belonged to the south of the county and had moved to town that day with his family, his father having taken up some new form of employment for the local council. As we talked I could not help but notice he had an eye for the girls, ogling all that passed. When he moved on I asked Danny if he had noticed how the girls had responded to his winks and wisecracks.

"I did indeed," said he.

"Do you think he's got it, whatever it is?" I asked.

"I'm sure he has and if we play our cards right we'll soon have it too."

We determined to cultivate the acquaintance and make the stranger feel that he was among friends. Our first, brief encounter had revealed to our eagle eyes that hidden within that rustic's frame was the secret of successful seduction. We wondered if he was fully aware of it himself having never before been in the midst of so much pulchritude, but it was our avowed aim to corral and hog-tie him before he became hopelessly enamoured with one of the local fillies. For more than a week we never saw hair nor hide of him, it was as if he had never been, that we had both shared the same dream. When I did meet him it was during the middle of the day and I was on my own. He looked such a mess I nearly passed by without recognition.

"Hello Sean, haven't seen you for a bit, where have you been?" I asked cheerily.

"Do I know you?" he asked.

"Of course you do. Weren't you talking to myself and Danny on your first night in town?"

"Oh yes, I remember. Ah, I've been very busy up at the house. I'm just down for some more paint now."

"So that's what you're at? You look like you're painting yourself."

I thought it was time to terminate the small-talk so I came straight to the point.

"How about giving yourself a break and coming to the pictures with us tonight?"

"That would be nice; where will I meet you?"

I was about to say "under the town clock", but that, I remembered, would be a rather dangerous place to leave him waiting in view of its popularity as a place of romantic assignment.

"We'll meet you outside Booley's at quarter to nine."

"Where is that?" he asked.

"It's the gent's toilet at the bottom of town. You can't miss it, your nose will take you there."

That first night was the foundation stone on which we had planned to build the relationship; the cementing of a friendship that Danny and I intended to foster while there was something to be gained from it. We held him in tight rein on that and on successive nights while we worked out a plan of campaign. We had to be certain that his conquests when they occurred would have to be in our presence and that none would amount to anything more than a one-night stand. It was only from careful study of his *modus operandi* we could hope to learn anything. A week of careful nurturing of his trust and confidence had passed before we were confident we could let him off the leash to demonstrate the know-how we were confident he possessed.

Our first trials were on the main street promenade where we excited his libido with tales of our own fictional conquests, which we backed up with lurid details of the sexual appetites of some of the parading crumpet. Our verbal incitement had the effect of an aphrodisiac that sent him into action with astonishing alacrity: like a wing-footed Mercury he had vanished with his willing victim before we or her companions had any idea of what was happening.

Our only recourse now was to put plan "B" into action. This involved contacting him before he kept any date that we suspected he might commit himself to in the heat of a passionate embrace. We could not permit him to have a steady, at least not until we had wormed his secret out of him.

He was surprised to find us on his doorstep shortly after tea on the following evening.

"We're just off for a bit of sea air," said Danny. "Want to come along?"

"Well as a matter of fact I've got a date on," he answered, confirming our suspicions.

I took it on myself to fire off the first volley in the plan B campaign.

"Not with that thing you went off with last night?"

"What do you mean by that crack?" he asked sharply.

"Hold on now, don't get upset; we're your friends, we

141

only want to help," said Danny. "Get your jacket on," he
continued, "we'll put you wise to that one."

"Leave this to me," Danny whispered as Sean went to
fetch his coat. "You're too blunt; you nearly upset him."

The first part of our stroll was devoted to general small-
talk and it was not until we were walking along the canal
bank that Danny broached the subject of romance.

"How did you get on last night anyway?" he asked by
way of an opener.

"Not too bad, I'm taking her to the pictures tonight,"
said Sean proudly.

"I don't know how to say this," said Danny, "but if I
were you I wouldn't bother."

"Why not? What's wrong with her?"

"Sure she's a bloody old bag," answered Danny at his
diplomatic best.

If it were not for my quick intervention Danny would
have wound up in the canal, such was the rage that came
over Sean. That he restrained himself from the use of violence spoke volumes for his self-control, but it took several
minutes of soft wheedling on my part before he relaxed his
grip on Danny's neck-piece.

"He didn't mean any harm, he was only telling you the
truth," I told him from a safe distance. "You're a stranger
here and can't be expected to know what's what."

Continuing with our walk we filled him in with the sor-
did details relating to the character of his mavourneen,
and by the time we were leaning on the lock-gate where
the canal joined the bay we had convinced him he had
held in his arms the greatest trollop since Jezebel.

On the return journey we elicited from him the promise
that he would make no more hasty moves; that he would
play all future hands slowly and with our prior approval.
Though he kept his word and gave us prior warning of
whom he had targeted for his attentions, he picked up the
birds as easily as the feathered variety picked berries

from the bush, leaving us as bemused and ignorant as when we had started out. It wasn't that he ever said anything of exceptional interest; there were even times when he never uttered a word, but the end result was always the same: he got the girls and we got the glares.

"It must be the light," said Danny.

"What's wrong with the light?" I asked, puzzled.

"He doesn't say any magic words, does he? So he must have some secret sign that we can't see in this poor streetlight."

"There's not much we can do about that, is there?"

"There is: we can take him to a dance. The light's better there so we can watch his moves," explained Danny.

"I'm not much of a dancer and you know that, so what's the point?"

"So much the better," said Danny. "Besides you might learn while you're there."

"I don't know," I said, "but if you think it'll work I'll give it a try."

We put the proposition to him the following night and he turned it down flat on two counts: he didn't dance and he didn't have a decent suit.

"Well I'm no Fred Astaire," said I, "but at least I try."

"And if a suit is all that is stopping you, there is a lovely suit out at our house that my uncle left when he went to America that I'm sure would fit you," Danny offered.

"I don't know," came the reply, "I'm not all that keen on dancing."

"Balls to the dancing," said Danny. "Think of all the crumpet."

That was the clincher, and the next day I accompanied Sean out to Danny's place for the fitting. The suit was a tweed, dark green in colour but a little dated in style. Not that Sean noticed; to him a suit was a suit, and he wasn't going to look a gift-horse in the mouth. Rather shyly he retired behind a curtain to change, and when he reappeared I was taken aback. I suppose if I had bumped into him on some grouse-moor sometime around the turn of the century, with a shotgun under his arm and a retriever at his heels, I wouldn't have given him a second glance. But this was another time and another place and he looked as if he had just stepped out of H. G. Wells's time machine.

"Very nice," said Danny, "fits you like a glove."

The lad accepted the compliment as avidly as a starving dog would take a pork-chop.

"Yeah, I like it, it feels good; how much do you want for it?"

"Want for it?" Danny was shocked. "Want for it? Now that's poor form Sean. Sure if I wanted money for it I'd have sold it long ago."

"There's only one thing wrong, if you don't mind me saying, Sean," I chipped in. "You need a different pair of shoes; scruffed black doesn't go with tweeds."

"These are the only pair I've got," he sighed. "Wouldn't they be OK if I polished them?"

"No, of course not. You need a nice brown shoe to set that off."

"I can't afford a new pair of shoes just to go to a dance," he moaned.

"I think you're in luck again," I said, "because I know where there is a spanking pair going for only ten bob."

"A pair of shoes for only ten shillings? I can't see that."

"You're not in the bog now," I reassured him. "They are shop-soiled but you'll not know the difference. If they fit you, you're quids in."

"Do you think he'll really go dancing in that rig-out?" I asked Danny when Sean had left the room to change back into his old clothes.

"He'd go in bloody plus-fours if he got them for nothing," replied Danny laughing.

Bundling his new clothes up in old newspaper, Sean followed me out and we made our way back to town where I took him to the shop in which I had seen the cheap shoes. They were still lying in the window behind the ten bob price-tag.

"They have no lace-holes," he complained.

"Of course not, they're slip-ons," I explained. "Just go in and try them on, and if they fit buy 'em."

"You look as smart as a well-scraped carrot," I remarked when we met outside the dance-hall. "You'll certainly score tonight."

"I'm not too happy about the shoes. The soles are very thin."

"What do you expect for ten bob?" asked Danny. "Brogues?"

The hall was rather crowded, the women outnumbering the men by about five to one. We took up position not far from the door, from where we did a little form study. I could not help but notice that we had become a focus of attraction for the groups of females that stood around waiting for the invitation to dance. I had no objection to the glances; it was the whispered remarks behind mouth-shielding hands and the sly giggles that troubled me. I felt like high-tailing it out of there but when Danny strode in among them, selected a partner and took to the floor, my fears subsided. I turned my attention to Sean, remembering the reason we had come here. He appeared to have taken root, and when I enquired why he wasn't going into action he explained that he was unable to manage the quickstep and would prefer to wait until the band struck up a waltz.

When the moment arrived he was off like a shot towards a large group of clacking females who, as one, moved aside to offer him free passage, like the Red Sea parting before Moses. Girl partnered girl to swing away in time to the music, leaving Sean as bewildered as a fox in a hastily vacated chicken-coop.

"Don't worry," I sympathised when he returned disconsolately. "It's because you're a stranger; wait till they get used to you."

We had backed a loser. There was nothing further to be gained from the association. The lad was a charlatan whose earlier successes had been nothing more than beginner's luck, to which we had mistakenly attributed mysterious powers. The answer to our problem would have to be sought elsewhere than in the company of a recently arrived clod-hopper. To be fair, we owed him some measure of gratitude, because if we had not gone to that dance we might never have found what we had been seeking. For both Danny and me the night had a satisfactory conclusion. The pale moon smiled benignly as we kissed goodnight to our fair companions, as if it knew that we had discovered the secret of success in flirtation and romance.

I went to the dance alone on the following Saturday night, confidently assured of further success in the love stakes.

"Where is your friend of last week?" asked my blue-eyed partner of the fox-trot.

"Which one do you mean, Danny or Sean?"

"I don't know the name," she replied. "I mean the nut in the Donegal tweeds and carpet slippers."

The Blackberry Picker

I T WAS FRANK who talked me into it. It was during the "Emergency" and a few weeks previously he had enlisted in Ireland's part-time army, the Local Defence Force.

I met him as he was making his way to a training session. He looked rather smart in his green uniform and like a convert to a new religion he was bubbling over with enthusiasm. Determined to spread the gospel of patriotism he seized his opportunity to try yet again to inveigle me into becoming a disciple of his new creed. He talked to me of Ireland and her need; he cut no ice. He spoke about the defence of freedom and democracy; he received the cold shoulder. He enthused on the camaraderie and friendship in the force; he got the thumbs down. He dropped a veiled hint of an annual camp somewhere down by the sea; he got the thumbs up and a new convert. Of smaller stature than I, he had difficulty keeping up with me as I hurried to the training hall to get my name down for a free holiday.

I was signed on immediately and was ushered over to a corner to join a few more raw recruits where we spent the remainder of the evening learning the difference between both sides of our anatomies. The following week it was assumed that we could now make the distinction between left and right so we moved on to lesson two – how to walk. To assist us in this difficult manoeuvre our instructor risked permanent damage to his vocal chords as he bawled out the sequence in which we should move our feet to achieve locomotion. I strode home elated that night and proudly marched up and down the kitchen to impress the family with my new knowledge and ability.

I may have impressed my family, but it took several weeks for my superiors to accept that I was worthy of a uniform. When I finally satisfied them that I could put one foot in front of the other without tripping up they issued me with a chit to take along to the quartermaster's store where I would be measured and kitted out. The store was situated in the centre of town and the man in charge was a member of the regular army. He ran the place as if it were a shop; nine to five, with an hour for lunch. He had a strong aversion to amateur soldiers and an intense dislike of being disturbed during his rest period, which also happened to be from nine to five with an hour for lunch.

He didn't have time to open his newspaper next morning before I slapped my chit on the counter and stood to attention to await measurement. He threw a cursory glance at the chit, leaned over the counter, eyed me from head to toe and asked:

"What size?"

"What size what?"

"What size boots do you wear?"

"I don't know, I've never worn boots."

"Oh my God, another one. Well what size shoes do you wear?"

"Nines."

He turned his back impatiently, took a greatcoat down from a shelf and laid it on the counter. From various shelves and boxes he collected the rest of the gear, piling it in a heap on the coat which he folded over before passing a ledger across the counter and pressing a pen into my hand.

"Sign here," he growled.

"What if they don't fit?" I asked, scribbling my signature.

"They'll fit."

There was no alternative but to take his word for it, though, judging by the number of ill-fitting uniforms I had seen down at the drill-hall, I didn't hold out much hope. I rushed home, went straight to the bedroom and did a quick-change act. Surveying myself in the wardrobe mirror I was greeted with a vision of how Stan Laurel might look in Oliver Hardy's clothes; the entire outfit would have looked better had it been wrapped around a broom-handle. If war came to our shores I might very well be killed in this outfit, but I had no intention of being seen dead in it, so I plucked up some courage and took it back.

"You again? What's up now?"

"They don't fit," I said, passing him the bundle.

"Who told you that?"

"Nobody told me, I could see for myself," I replied rather sharply.

"So we want our uniforms tailor-made now, do we? I'm afraid you're out of luck; take 'em and go."

"Put a couple of holes in this then," I snapped back, grabbing the beret and pulling it down over my head. "At least I'll be able to see where I'm going."

Reluctantly he accepted the evidence of his own eyesight and exchanged everything. No believer in miracles, I wasn't too disappointed to find that the second outfit was no perfect fit, but I was thankful at least that it clung to me a little more closely.

Now that we were looking like soldiers we were considered capable of bearing arms and were duly issued with rifles. The Remington .303 had, we were told, seen service with the American army on the Western Front. It looked ancient enough to have been in use with the US 7th Cavalry and to be a relic of the battle of the Little Big Horn. Of great weight, and issued without ammunition, I thought we might be expected to use it as a shillelagh; as such, in close combat it would have had a devastating effect upon any enemy. Carting it around worked wonders on my physique, enlarging and strengthening my muscles and transforming me from a weedy boy into a reasonably well-built young man. While having no respect for it as a firearm I would have no hesitation in recommending it as an excellent aid to physical development.

Eventually our training took us beyond the confines of the drill-hall, out onto the firing-range, on route marches and into mock battles over rough terrain. We learned how to make cocktails of the Molotov variety, the art of camouflage, and how to lay an ambush. It was on one of the latter exercises that I came in close contact with the old lady who heard voices from beyond the grave, if not the voice of God Himself.

It was Saturday morning when word came through that the enemy was approaching the town from the direction of Killarney, where they had been sampling the tourist attractions. To protect our homes and womenfolk from alien depredation we were to set an ambush a few miles outside town. The site chosen was a straight stretch of road, bordered on both sides by narrow verges of long grass, shallow ditches and dense whitethorn hedges. Spreading out and rolling into the ditches we concealed ourselves, breaking our outlines by partially covering our persons with grass and twigs. I found myself situated close to a small cross set in a concrete plinth that marked the spot where some unfortunate had met his death during the War of Independence. Silently and invisibly we watched the cars, carts and cycles pass by, their drivers and passengers unaware of our presence.

The donkey-cart that pulled over on the verge and came to a halt beside me was driven by its sole occupant – a little old lady dressed in a grey shawl and wearing voluminous, black, ankle-length skirts. She sat for a moment looking up and down the road and when she was satisfied that all was clear she hurried on to the verge and squatted near my feet. I heard the rustle of clothes as she raised her skirts. As I slowly and quietly withdrew my feet from the site of the expected deluge I heard the sepulchral tones of the fellow lying a few feet behind me.

"Not on hallowed ground, my child."

The old lady froze for a moment, jumped up quicker than if she had squatted on a nettle, glanced all about her, made the sign of the cross and bolted for the cart. The poor donkey was startled out of her wits as the stick made contact with her back and she shot off like a two-year-old filly. Like a demented sadist, the little old lady flogged the hide of the unfortunate animal, speeding her up and over the hill without once looking back.

I had been one of the country's part-time defenders for several months now and the time for the annual two-week holiday was drawing close. Speculation was rife; practically every man in the company had inside information on where this year's camp would be held. From Bundoran, around the coast to Tramore, every resort of any merit was mentioned as our likely destination. I was surprised at how many of my comrades had relations of high military rank who had the power and influence to decide the location of our holiday. I had no high-ranking relatives, neither did I voice any preferences; I would be quite satisfied with any location as long as it was over the hill and far away. When the official notification was finally posted up it shook me rigid and tempted me to burn my uniform in protest: we were to holiday on the other side of the wall at the bottom of our garden – the local army barracks. Months of diligent training to earn a well-deserved break at some famous resort and I found myself rewarded with a close-up view of the far side of our garden wall.

I was sat in the kitchen sulking when Frank arrived all spruced up, his rifle slung over his shoulder and his kitbag on his back. He looked as if he were about to set out on safari.

"Aren't you ready?" he enquired.

"I'm not bloody going," I barked.

"Why not? It'll be great fun."

"I'll tell you why not. All my bloody life I've been looking at that bloody wall and I'm not going on holiday to view the other side of it!"

My mother, coming in from the garden, quickly grasped the gist of the conversation.

"If you're not going there are a few jobs I've got for you," she said. "The garden badly needs weeding, and. . ."

"Hang on a minute while I get ready," I called to Frank as he turned to go.

We signed in and found the men of our own company among the hundreds milling around on the parade ground. The laughter and small-talk created a holiday atmosphere that washed away my depression and disillusionment and injected me with fresh enthusiasm. With head erect, shoulders squared and chest expanded I listened attentively to the commanding officer who had just descended from his ivory tower to welcome us to his domain. He complimented us on our turn-out, lavished praise on us for our dedication and patriotism and expressed the hope that during our stay we would behave like good soldiers and prove to be a credit to the uniform. Bringing his little homily to a close he gave me the feeling that he had doubts about our being properly house-trained when he informed us that we were to be segregated from his own men. While they slept in barracks or billets we were to be put out to grass. Not for us the comfort of four walls and a roof over our heads; we were to have nothing more substantial than a bit of thin canvas to protect us from the elements. We were privileged to be patriots but patriotism provided no privileges.

Military men seem to be obsessed with uniformity. To

the martial mind there is no such thing as individuality; men must dress alike, walk alike, even think alike. I suppose that it wouldn't do to have anything less than automatons to wage a war with any hope of success. The regular army's success rate in moulding the minds of men was extremely high, due no doubt to the severe punishments it had licence to dish out to nonconformists, but with our part-time warriors there was a different story to tell. At our regular training sessions where our numbers were comparatively small very few disciplinary problems arose, but when hundreds of men and lads from vastly different walks of life were thrown together for a couple of weeks it was a recipe for chaos.

Everything started out well on that first afternoon; our intentions were good and we really meant to behave like soldiers, but as with all the plans of mice and men ours fared no better than those of Robbie Burns's day. Our two-man tents were laid out in neat rows in regulation order. Frank and I had decided to doss down together, and it was a couple of weary lads who crawled under the blankets when the daylight failed. At first I paid little heed to the sound of the mallet as someone drove home his pegs. There are some men of such pessimistic nature that they wear a belt as reinforcement to their braces, and maybe we had one such in our midst who worried about the supports to his bivouac. As the hammering ceased and I turned over, thankful for the silence, another nut started his capers, and then from the opposite direction a third.

"It sounds like we're surrounded by screwballs," I whispered across to Frank.

If he had intended to reply he didn't get the chance because as I finished speaking, like the little pig's house our canvas shelter came crashing down around our ears.

When we crawled out from beneath our collapsed abode the sight that greeted us was one of total devastation. The place looked as if it had been visited by a tornado; hardly a tent stood erect. Half-naked men were running about hell-bent on destruction, as if afflicted by some form of mass hysteria. Wrapping our blankets over our shoulders Frank and I sat down and waited for our clouded brains to clear before attempting to re-erect our shelter. We did not have long to wait; within minutes an army sergeant with a couple of his men arrived to restore order and patrolled the site until every man-jack was calmed down and safely tucked up in his blankets. A peace descended on the camp as if a truce had been signed but, alas, it was one that was written on water. My heart missed a few beats when I heard it again – the dull and ominous thud of mallet on peg. The phantom leveller had struck again, lighting the spark that would re-kindle the flames of a monomania that would raze the camp to the ground. This time I didn't wait for the inevitable but rushed out to pull up every peg in sight, our own included; the bug had bitten me and I was all but foaming at the mouth as I sought vengeance for deprivation of sleep. The return of the guard brought only temporary respite: the night was fated to be one of sleeplessness and dawn found me on the verge of exhaustion, collapsed upon our tent with a peg tightly gripped in one hand and a mallet grasped in the other.

I have no recollection as to how I managed to drag myself through the following day. For the first time in my life I had endured twenty-four hours without sleep and I was both physically and mentally shattered. I was isolated from reality behind glazed eyes; my brain was a vacuum into which the sounds of the outside world wandered to die of suffocation. That I stood, moved or responded to orders could only be attributed to the manipulations of a heavenly puppeteer because there was no chance that my body could be controlled by a loaf on which had been hung an "out of order" sign.

That night I must have grabbed some sleep because when I opened my eyes it had grown dark. How long I had been curled up I could not say. Recollection of retiring had vanished like some long past, insignificant dream. I lay quietly, listening to the sounds that had disturbed me; these were not the dull thumps of wood on wood that had plagued the camp the night before, this was the pitter-patter of raindrops enjoying a céilí on the taut canvas. The rhythm soon had a soothing effect upon me, becoming a monotonous sleep-inducing lullaby that still worked its somnolent magic even when the choreographer brought on the clog-dancers.

"For God's sake wake up!" Frank pleaded as he shook my shoulder.

"What's the bloody matter now?" I snarled. "Am I never to get any sleep?"

"There's water coming in; my bed's soaking," he moaned.

Quickly gathering my wits together I discovered he was not on his own; our "biscuits" were miniature islands in a couple of inches of water. I fumbled in the dark for my clothes to find them as waterlogged as if they were sponges; I had seen my mother pegging out far drier clothes on one of her wash-days.

Squatting together with what dry blankets we could salvage wrapped around our chilled bodies we listened to the incessant rattle of the rain on our flimsy shelter and watched the water lapping like an incoming tide around our little island. The sound of voices wavering through the saturated air told us our neighbours were faring no better than ourselves; we were all in the same boat.

Our misery was ended when the order came through to abandon ship and make for the gymnasium where we found dry bedding had been laid out in readiness through the entire length of the building and I quickly selected a position near the centre of the floor where I threw myself down in the expectation of at least a few more hours kip. My expectations fell far short of reality. With the departure of the officers and the call for lights out bedlam erupted. I found myself in the unfortunate position of being a minority of one in a room full of insomniacs. Like children let loose in a play-field everybody went crazy: pillow fights, wrestling matches and friendly races up and down the aisles I tried to ignore, but when some lunatic produced a football I surrendered to despair.

I was so exhausted that despite the mayhem I managed to get an odd minute's sleep, but nowhere near enough for my needs, and when I heard during the day that we were to be properly billeted I sighed with relief and promised myself that straight after tea I would crawl into bed and sleep till bugle-call. It was a nicely laid out billet, two rows of beds, about twenty in all and in the centre of the floor a stove for winter heating. Each billet was to be under the control of an NCO so that there would be no repetition of the previous two nights' capers, and for that I was thankful.

I had finally achieved a good night's sleep but it didn't seem to have bestowed on me any feelings of well-being; on the contrary, I awoke feeling all washed up and out of sorts. Instead of invigoration my holiday was having a debilitating effect upon me; I felt as if I were on a downhill slide into utter exhaustion from which I saw no hope of recovery, and only three days into my long-awaited vacation. I found it impossible to face breakfast and as the day dragged on I felt my energy slip away until by teatime I could hardly lift my feet. I sat in the mess toying with my food when I felt the first flush of a temperature. It lasted only momentarily but brought beads of sweat to my brow. I wrote it off as due to the heat of the day and the stuffiness of the mess-hall, but when it suddenly rose again and Frank, who was sitting across the table from me, remarked on my lack of colour I had to admit that I was running a fever.

"You'd better report sick," said Frank in concern. "You

don't look very well to me."

Taking his advice I made my way to sick-bay.

"What do you want?" snapped the orderly.

"I don't feel very well," I whispered apologetically.

"Report on sick parade in the morning," he barked dismissively.

"I feel sick now."

"You can't come barging in here anytime of the day saying you're sick. This is the army, you can only be sick in the morning, the doctor will see you then."

By now the sweat was pouring out of me, whether through fever or frustration I wasn't sure but I felt that if he didn't do something quickly I'd collapse.

"Well, can't you at least take my temperature?" I pleaded.

He put his book down and slowly rose from his chair, went to a cabinet, found a thermometer, gave it a vigorous shake and stuffed it in my mouth.

"Good God, you are ill," he said as he took the reading, his eyes popping. "Get undressed and into bed quick."

I needed no second telling. I began to feel better the minute I slid between the cool, clean linen sheets. It was worth being sick to have the prospect of a quiet night in a soft, comfortable bed. As the orderly disappeared on some mysterious errand I luxuriated in my new-found comfort, regretting I hadn't reported sick as soon as I entered the camp.

"When last did your bowels move?" enquired the orderly after he had been through all the formalities of name, address and next of kin.

"Don't know," I answered truthfully.

"What do you mean? Have you been today?"

"No, not today."

"Have you been yesterday or the day before?"

"No."

"Have you been this last week then? Can you give me

some bloody idea when?"

"To be honest I can't remember, but it's been a long time. It must have been a couple of weeks ago," I croaked, trying my best to be helpful.

"You will have to have an enema then; that's your trouble, your bowels need clearing."

"That's OK," I said as he turned to leave, thinking to myself that an enema was the army version of a dose of senna.

I was slightly puzzled when he returned wheeling a trolley full of strange-looking gear; it seemed an elaborate ritual to administer a simple laxative. When he told me to turn on my side, expose my bum and shove it over the edge of the bed I thought he had taken leave of his senses.

"Hold on a minute, we're having no shennanigans here; I've heard about your kind. I'm getting out of here. I'm going to report you!"

He pushed me back on the bed and explained the reason for his strange request.

"Your bowels are set like concrete; it might take a stick of dynamite to shift you but we'll try this first. Now turn over and do as you're told."

I thanked God he didn't have to resort to such drastic action as inserting a stick of dynamite where he had now inserted the nozzle clipped to the end of the rubber tube he had brandished sadistically as he explained the benefits of an injection of soapy water. I squealed for mercy as he began the pumping action. I felt that he had taken advantage of my trust to deceive me, inserting the carbolic in solid rather than liquid form. I was thinking it might have been more humane to have used the explosive when he suddenly pulled the plug on me and my innards fell out. At least that was what I thought. I felt as I imagined a balloon might do when punctured – deflated and spent. Washed, and refreshed with a cup of strong hot tea, I turned over and dropped into a long undisturbed sleep.

I was awakened with a gentle shake from the same orderly who had tended me the previous evening. My temperature had dropped slightly and, feeling much better already, I expected to be discharged by the doctor when he called to have a gander at me. When he did arrive his first words filled me with dread.

"How long have you had that rash?"

"What rash?"

"That rash all over your face and body."

I looked down at my chest and arms: I was covered in red blotches that I knew had nothing to do with measles.

"I didn't have it when I came in; I must have picked it up here," I said nervously.

"We had better get you to hospital straight away. I'll make the necessary arrangements."

He left hurriedly, as if he were afraid of contagion, and left me wondering what in hell I was harbouring. I expected the ambulance men to arrive wearing masks but my fears were proved groundless, though they wasted no time bundling me onto a stretcher and carting me out of the building. It was only a short haul to the county hospital and when we sped past the entrance my worries increased.

"Where are you going?" I called to the driver. "You've passed the hospital."

"We're taking you to Mallow," he replied.

"I must be bad," I thought to myself. "What's wrong that they are taking me that far?"

What was so special about Mallow? What rare and exotic ailment would warrant taking me out of my own county? Were the germs of my disease so virulent that I was going to be used as a weapon to decimate the population of the county of Cork? The same thing had been done before to wipe out others of the earth's primitive tribes; why not again? I tortured myself with such questions before I plucked up courage to ask for the truth.

"Why Mallow?"

"Because that's where the nearest military hospital is," replied the driver.

Soon I was tucked up in bed by two attractive young nurses who fussed and fawned over me as if I were a curly-headed baby. I was being spoiled and I lay back to enjoy the experience, feeling better than I had done for days and praying my stay would be a long one. My mother could not have been more attentive to me than my ministering angels, and the situation didn't alter with the change of shift. With lights-out I cast the events of the past few days behind me and turned in to dream that I was an Arabian sultan with my own private harem.

"Have your bowels moved this morning?" asked the masculine-looking matron on her morning tour of inspection.

"Not yet matron," I replied.

"An enema," she ordered the attendant nurse.

"I had one yesterday before I was sent here," I protested, hoping to put her off.

"An enema," she repeated as she moved off to the next bed.

"Good God Almighty, save me, work one of your miracles – do something; do anything, but bloody get me out of this," I prayed.

Maybe I was asking too much of Him; maybe He had His hands full with a world war on. Whatever it was He ignored me, abandoning me to my fate.

"Have you had a movement this morning?" enquired the matron on the following day's ward visit.

"Yes matron," I lied. I was prepared to die of constipation and risk damnation as a liar rather than suffer another internal carbolic scouring. I had resolved that from then on any liquids that entered my body would do so through the orifice that nature had provided for the purpose.

Within a week I was up and about and free to wander

about the hospital grounds dressed in "hospital blues" – a lightweight jacket and trousers that all patients were obliged to wear. If I was improving in health I was also improving financially. I was the lucky recipient of funds from two sources. The payment that I would have received had I not taken ill was forwarded on to me, and the army in its benevolence allotted me a similar amount so that, all in all, I wasn't doing too badly. Of course I was still plagued with the old trouble: money had an allergy to me. It tended to burn a hole in my pocket and fill me with restlessness in its desire to escape. There was no way I could relieve myself of the torture within the confines of the hospital and I didn't yet qualify for a pass to go into town. I explained my problem to one of my new-found friends.

"Your troubles are over; we'll go blackberry picking tomorrow."

"You misunderstand me; I don't want blackberries, I want to spend some money."

"You'd be surprised what you can spend blackberry picking around here," he replied with a wink.

The following day after lunch he came up and shoved a tin can in my hand and told me to get my greatcoat and cap and not to forget my money; he was taking me blackberry picking. I strolled with him up the hill to the hedge where several other patients were busy filling cans with succulent black fruit. We slowly worked along the hedge, I looking for the best while my friend made no distinction between green, red or black. Watching him, I thought he was either colour blind or a nut-case or worse still a colour blind nut-case. Despite my concern for the mental state of my companion I was aware that the horde of fruitpickers was quickly and mysteriously diminishing. At a point farther along the hedge they vanished one by one as if the earth had opened up and swallowed them. Close to the dematerialization zone I turned from stripping a heavily laden bramble to find myself alone: my companion had melted into thin air.

"Drop that can and get to hell out of there," I heard his voice from the other side of the seemingly impenetrable hedge.

"How do I get over there?" I asked.

"Get down and crawl through where that pile of cans is lying," came the instruction. Worming my way through to a rutted cart-track I saw my companion already on his way down the hill. Falling into step beside him I listened as he explained the reason for the subterfuge. For patients who wished to visit the town and failed to qualify for a pass, the way we had come was the only way of escaping without being seen. There were no restrictions on wandering around the grounds, and blackberrying was a good enough reason to explain overlong absence from the ward. He explained that if we became separated I was to keep a sharp eye out for "red caps" and that it was vital that I returned to the hospital the way we had come out. If I were found out without a pass I might find myself on Spike Island on a holiday I hadn't bargained for.

Regrettably I never saw the town of Mallow. The itinerary of my guided tour took me no farther than the first boozer on the approach road to the town where I was invited to wash the dust of the road from my throat.

"Two pints of Guinness," ordered my companion.

"I'll have lemonade," said I. "I don't drink."

"Don't drink? Good God!" He couldn't have been more shocked if I had told him I practised cannibalism.

"Ah, come on now, have a drop of cider then; you need something stronger than lemonade after what you've been through. It won't harm you a bit."

"All right then, I'll have one," I said rather reluctantly, "but only one."

One hour and three pints later I was gently helped out onto the road and faced in the direction of the hospital.

"Don't forget now, you've been picking blackberries," the

voice called after me as I stepped out on india-rubber legs.

I took a few hesitant steps forward, then stopped to prop myself against a wall to take stock of the situation. I checked out my brain first: it seemed to be working normally; it was aware of our location, our destination and the route to be followed. I then took a physical inventory and found everything to be in order. I mulled over the problem for several minutes before finally admitting to myself that I was inebriated, or, in more common parlance, stupidly drunk. Those were mighty potent blackberries, I told myself and started to laugh. The more I thought about it the more I laughed, until the tears ran down my cheeks.

I couldn't stand here laughing all day so I tried to move on. My legs developed a will of their own, taking me everywhere except where I wanted to go. Overriding the normal communication channels between brain and limbs I resorted to verbal instructions with some limited success. Laughing inanely I took the width of the road as I staggered towards my goal. Imbued with the fabled courage of the Dutch I contemptuously dismissed the idea of sneaking up the back lane like a thief in the night; instead I resolved to march through the main gate like a soldier and a man.

The car that quietly drew up beside me put paid to my plans of a full-frontal assault. It was a chauffeur-driven army vehicle containing two high-ranking officers. I assumed that the quantity of gold braid sported signified they ranked no lower than full-blown generals. Pulling myself together I stood as smartly to attention as my condition would allow and gave a good impression of a salute. Lowering a window the nearest general stuck his head out and enquired if I were going to the hospital.

"I am, shur," I slurred respectfully, knowing my place in the pecking order.

"Jump in and take the load off your feet," he ordered

kindly.

It was an order easier issued than executed. I opened the back door to hop in beside the brass only to have it snatched out of my hand and loudly slammed, followed by a curt order to get in beside the driver. Leaning against the car for support I tried to move forward, but found my coat had been trapped in the hastily closed door. I shoved my head through the open window and laughingly spluttered into the general's face, "My coat's tlapped, shur."

His face reddened slightly and he pushed me away, quickly opened the door and released my coat. The walk in the fresh air had further intoxicated me and I was aware of a rapid deterioration in my condition. I fumbled with the handle of the front door but found its mechanics beyond the limits of my capabilities. The driver leaned over and opened it from inside; I tumbled in, profuse in my expressions of gratitude. I had trouble trying to close the door behind me, and were it not for the quick thinking and fast action of the driver in grabbing my shoulder I would have found myself kissing the surface of the road.

"How long have you been in hospital?" asked the second general.

"Nearly chew weeks, shur," I replied, turning around and leaning over the back of the seat.

"Been to town, have you?" enquired the first one.

"Oh no, shur," I said, shaking my head so vigorously my cap slipped down over my eyes.

"I'sh bin blackberry picking, shur."

As we drove through the entrance I returned the salute of the sentry as if I too were of high rank. When the car drew up outside the main building I managed to undo the door-catch without assistance. I slid out onto my feet, keeping myself upright by clutching doggedly to the car. As far gone as I was I didn't forget my manners, so I stuck my head back in and said, "Shanks for the lift lads."

Loosening my grip on the car I suddenly lost my balance

and fell back onto the drive. Struggling helplessly to rise I was overcome by another fit of hysterical laughter, and as I glimpsed the expressions on the faces of the two generals the realisation dawned on me that if I had any hopes of a military career they were dashed to destruction on the gravel drive of a hospital outside the town of Mallow.

The Botch

HOW MANY TIMES does one hear it said that one's
schooldays are the best days of one's life? I have
heard that statement made so often and by so
many people that I sometimes wonder why it wasn't so
with me. Schooldays were no picnics, though I do not deny
that they very well might have been were it not for the
fact that I was compelled to actually attend school.

I was in my fifth year of life and enjoying myself very
nicely when the novelty of having children running around
the house, getting under her feet and tugging at her skirt,
wore off my mother. She scraped together a few bob, purchased a cheap satchel, stuffed it with a few pencils and
sheets of writing paper, slung it over my shoulder and
bundled me out the door into the hands of a section of soci-
ety that for several years were to be the bane of my life.

I have very little recollection of my first few years of
schooling, but the memories I do have are pleasurable, in
stark contrast to those of young Danny who started his
schooling at about the same time as I though at a different
establishment. The mental scars of his experience have
stayed to haunt him for the rest of his life, and to this day
he can still graphically describe what befell him when he
innocently brought up the subject of sex in a class of six-
year-olds.

One of his young classmates had lost a front tooth over
the weekend, and on arrival at school on Monday morning

became the butt of several childish jokes. Danny passed the remark that losing a front tooth was the penalty boys had to pay for kissing girls. The statement caused uproarious laughter among the group of inquisitive gogglers gathered around the hapless victim of childish waggishness. The teacher, a humourless nun of severe countenance and stiff demeanour, entered the room at the height of the laughter.

"Please may I ask what we find so amusing?" she enquired of nobody in particular.

No classroom ever existed that did not contain at least one crawling sniveller of a teacher's pet.

"Danny sez Liam lost a tooth 'cos he's bin kissin' girls," piped up one such toady.

Had he said that Father Matthew of temperance fame had been a secret imbiber he could not have caused greater shock. The blood drained from the nun's face and for a moment it looked as if she might collapse in a dead faint on top of her informant. Pulling herself together she charged across the room to throw herself in a prostrate heap before a statue of the Virgin Mary. For a few minutes she lay motionless and silent in prayer, then, slowly rising to her knees, she blessed herself and raised her arms in supplication.

"Please God, guide me; what am I to do?" she prayed aloud.

She went on to explain to the Almighty that the Evil One had entered her classroom and taken possession of the body of young Danny. The vile spirit would have to be exorcised without delay if her whole class were not to be robbed of their souls. So emotional had she become and so eloquent her prayer that the silent onlookers dropped to their knees and crossed themselves; all, that is, except Danny, who stood wondering what in hell was going on. This was his second mistake of the morning because the devout one, on turning her head to see him standing alone among his kneeling companions, took it as an act of satanic defiance. Fortified by the divine acknowledgement of her prayers and doggedly determined to deliver young Danny from the evil clutches of Old Nick she jumped to her feet and stumbled across the room to her desk. Opening a drawer and extracting a vicious-looking strop she paused for only a moment to draw a deep breath before bearing down on her possessed pupil, grabbing one of his wrists in a talon-like hand and setting out to beat the living daylights and the devil out of him. Alternating between one hand and another she continued her ritual of exorcism until she was near collapse from physical exhaustion. The cries and tears of the host to the horned intruder were ignored as she staggered breathlessly from the room to summon reinforcements.

It was a younger and stronger bride of Christ who took up the strop on behalf of goodness and light, and it was not until they were both satisfied that the Prince of Darkness had departed for the comparative peace and painlessness of the bottomless pit that they put aside the leather. But Danny's troubles were not yet over; like a pariah he was to be segregated from the others of his class. To the holy ones there was something badly amiss in a lad whose person could so easily fall prey to an evil spirit. His classmates were forbidden to associate with him under pain of mortal sin until the exorcism had been confirmed by a priest.

I was more fortunate than Danny in my early contact with the teaching profession. My first school was what was known as national, having no connection with the religious teaching orders, though we did have a weekly visit from a priest who would spend a half-hour or so instructing us on the Faith. The severest punishment I was ever to receive at that particular school was the occasional sting of a birch on the palm of the hand, and then only when I deserved it. I respected my teachers, who were strict but fair and, on the whole, kindly. When my time came to leave I might have gone without a blemish on my record if it were not for one minor detail: I could not say the Lord's Prayer.

To be honest I could recite every prayer in the book when I was in need of divine assistance; the real trouble was my shortcomings as a linguist. There was no way I could master the Irish language, and prayers at school had to be said in the native tongue. I did a wonderful job of covering up. I stood erect at morning prayer opening and closing my mouth like a contented trout in the local stream, but all that ever emerged was pure gibberish. I had even invented my own gobbledegook that bore a remarkable resemblance to the real thing. I got away with it for ages and might have succeeded in bluffing my way through indefinitely had it not been for the preparations for Confirmation.

For a few weeks before the big day our education was concerned with religious instruction to the exclusion of all other subjects. If any student were to fail before the bishop it wouldn't be one from our school: that disgrace would never be lived down. Nobody had ever failed in the school's history and if our teachers had any say in the matter the record would remain intact. I knew they had nothing to worry about where I was concerned: I knew my catechism inside out and back to front; I knew as much about the four gospels as if I had written them myself; I was a font of religious knowledge that had sailed through many preliminary examinations and was a credit to my teacher.

"A piece of cake," thought I as the girl who was brought in to give us the final test fired off the questions to each of the lads in turn. Silently I answered each one correctly and eagerly awaited my turn to show her how clever I was.

"Say the Ár nAthar," she ordered.

"Who, me?" I asked in surprise.

"Yes, you."

"Our Father who art . . ."

"No: in Irish," she cut me off.

So it was true. There was an Almighty up there looking down on us; He had noted my bluff and was now calling it. How else could that girl be suddenly prompted to switch from asking questions from the catechism to asking someone to recite something as facile as the Lord's Prayer? Why, of all the class, did she pick on me? How was I going to wriggle out of this?

"Sure, that's too easy; ask me something hard."

She was powerless in the hands of her Maker; it was futile trying to put her off. With my hand over my mouth in the pretence of scratching my nose I mumbled my gibberish in rapid, hushed tones.

"I can't hear you. Slow down and speak louder," she commanded.

I was trapped. Nothing short of a sudden earthquake could save me now, and I knew very well the futility of silently praying for one of those catastrophes.

"You've made me forget it now," I said going into the attack.

"Miss, Miss," she shouted across to the teacher, "this lad can't say the Ár nAthar."

"Don't be so ridiculous," said the teacher, approaching with a smile on her face. "Everybody can say the Ár nAthar."

"This one can't," persisted the girl.

"Come on now; say the Ár nAthar for me, like a good boy," said the teacher firmly in a room full of hush.

"She made me forget it, shouting at me," I pleaded.

"Now, now, that won't do, nobody forgets the Ár nAthar. Come on, let's have it."

"I don't know it, Miss," I blurted out, conceding defeat.

"My God, I don't believe it! Only a few days from Confirmation and you don't know the Ár nAthar!" she almost screamed.

170

I was vaguely aware of the babble of excitement that swept through the room as she hurried out to inform the other members of the staff that she had discovered some form of heathen lurking in her class. Within minutes I was hauled away by the ear to face the headmaster. This was something he had never before come up against in his long career and he seemed at a loss as to how to handle it. He gazed at me for what seemed an eternity as if afraid to ask the vital question and have the answer confirm what he had already been told.

"Is it true that you cannot say the Ár nAthar?"

"'Tis sir."

"How did you manage to get away with it for so long?"

"I dunno, sir," which was true.

"It's too late to punish you now, but I'll tell you one thing: you'll know it before Saturday."

I was taken away to a little alcove where for the remainder of the week I had it rammed, crammed, stuffed and knocked into me, but it was labour in vain; I could not absorb it. They might as well have spent their time trying to fill a colander with water for all the success they had. As the week dragged on they became more desperate, even going so far as to suggest I should be held back until the following year. Had it not been that they were aware of the expense my mother had gone to to provide the new rig-out they might very well have done so.

I had never looked so smart as I did that morning when I marched up to the church accompanied by my proud mother, dolled out in my new suit, matching tie, shining shoes, socks nicely turned down just below the knees, white shirt, and with my hair neatly cut, combed and brilliantined. The teacher that met us at the door and took over control from my mother smiled benignly, showing none of the apprehension that she must have felt, grabbed me by the elbow and ushered me to my pew. Placing me as far as possible from the aisle between two of the biggest lads she could find she issued me with strict instructions to keep a very low profile. I had no alternative; she had also impressed upon my neighbours the need to keep me out of sight and they all but smothered me in their zeal.

I assume I was confirmed. I was certainly present during the ceremony; my teachers, family and friends showered me with congratulations and neighbours honoured the old tradition of lining my pockets in acceptance of the fact, but how it was achieved without seeing or being seen by the man in the mitre I couldn't understand. My two bodyguards did such a good job of hiding me from sight that I even took communion without seeing the priest who administered it and without him seeing whose tongue accepted the wafer. I had passed another milestone on the thoroughfare of life and before the year was out I was to move on to a more sophisticated educational establishment that was to inflict scars of the transient physical variety and, more importantly, permanent mental weals that were to alter forever my outlook on life and religion.

Long before I ever entered its doors the building filled me with foreboding; its dark-grey stone frontage, sombre green doors and cheerless windows radiated an aura of the Dickensian institution. When I stepped over the threshold I felt a strange kinship to Oliver Twist. I had heard many dark tales of the Brotherhood and their lack of understanding and compassion. Whether the stories I had heard were fact or fiction I did not know, but I was soon to find out. It might very well be some sort of record – though I didn't think to enquire – but I must have been the first pupil on his first day at school to have received a belting before being allotted a classroom. I was not the only new boy waiting in the hallway to be interviewed by the superior, but I was the only one to lean shoulder to the wall, legs crossed and hands in pockets. The only thing that differentiated me from the street-corner layabout was that I didn't have a fag hanging from my lower lip.

Unfortunately, the brother superior had got out of bed on the wrong side that morning and didn't take too kindly to my nonchalant stance, and wasted no time pulling out his chastiser and whipping a little more respectful decorum into me.

The way the teacher glanced at me after I had been introduced and the superior had taken him aside to whisper in his ear told me I was starting off with a tarnished reputation. I was left in no doubt as the day progressed and teachers of different subjects came and went but that I was marked out as a lad that had to be watched. I had passed through the hands of no less than four masters on that first day, two brothers and two lay teachers. It made a change from what I had been used to; being under the thumb of one tutor all and every day had been a bit of a drag, but it had the advantage that only one person dished out the homework. There should have been no problems about homework here, with only one or two extra subjects on the curriculum, but the trouble was that each and every one of my new teachers forgot that there were three others playing the same game.

I got through that first day without any more warming of the palms, but that was more than compensated for on day two, and again I brought it on myself. I always had a strong aversion to homework. To me enough valuable time was wasted in the classroom, so why should a lad be burdened with squandering the few short hours that remained of the day in useless learning? I collared a couple of likely looking prospects on the way home and outlined my plan: it was brilliant, and so simple I wondered why nobody had thought of it before. It might have worked too if we hadn't been so stupid as to copy each other's work verbatim. The odds against three lads working out a mathematical equation wrongly and arriving at the correct answer must be astronomical, though not beyond the bounds of possibility, but when the same three lads turn up on the very same day with three identical English essays it's stretching credulity to the utter limits.

I was overwhelmed by invitations to feel the texture and sample the effectiveness of a variety of scourging instruments. I didn't like to cause offence by displaying any preference so I cringed and wailed with equal abandon as the demonstrators grew almost apoplectic in their indignation and rage. I became the dog with the bad name, and from then on when anything went wrong in class I was the number one suspect as the mastermind at the bottom of it. My chastisement didn't prevent me from copying but it did teach me to indulge in a little variation; a few slaps for a mistake was always preferable to a damn good hiding for plagiarism.

I was never bottom of the class, but on the other hand I never climbed very high up the table and the greatest impediment to my progress was that all subjects were taught through the medium of Irish. I did muddle through and succeeded in passing on to the secondary school, but how anybody as dumb as I was and with such a tenuous grasp of the Irish language could have made that advance in his education is still one of the mysteries of my life.

I never made it through the first year in that third school: there was a limit to the brutality I was prepared to endure and when I had reached that limit I went out every morning, hid my satchel and took to the road until it was time to make tracks for home. It wasn't long before my mother had a letter enquiring as to why I was not attending classes; the cat was out of the bag. She said nothing to me for a couple of days but let me continue with the pretence.

"Why are you not going to school?" she asked when she thought the time was right.

I knew by the tone of her voice that there would be no point in denial.

"Because I can't take any more beatings."

"Beatings? What beatings?"

Then I told her how I had been suffering at the hands of one particular sadist. She found it hard to believe that what I told her was true; that any man wearing the garb of a Brother could indulge in such behaviour.

"I'm going to see him and get his side of the story," she assured me. "I'm sure that he hasn't given you any more than you deserve."

She was a woman who was a good judge of character, and after she had been to see the man of the thin lips, aquiline nose and hard, cold eyes she reached her own conclusion.

"He denied everything you said but I don't believe him. He has the look of the devil about him."

I don't know when she had set eyes on Old Nick but her brief contact with my tormentor had brought her firmly down on my side.

"Will you go to the tech if I can get you in?" she asked.

"Of course I will," I replied, pleased that I would never again see the inside of what for me had become a torture chamber.

I spent only two years in technical college but in those short months I learned more than I had done in all the other years put together. I felt that I was a human being again, not a punch-bag to satisfy the whims of frustrated sadists. To say that life had now become a bed of roses would be to lie. No halo ever defied gravity floating above my head, and where there was trouble I was usually to be found in the vicinity. I seemed to have a natural talent for getting into hot water and changing schools didn't change my aptitude for attracting misfortune of one kind or another.

The ultimate punishment for the real hard-case at the tech was expulsion; there was no room there for the persistent offender: you played the game according to the boss's rule or you got out. There was nothing more chastening for the recalcitrant than the humiliation of having to return after a parent had been down begging the headmaster for the re-instatement of a wayward offspring. In my two years at that school I had known of only two expulsions and both had been from my own class and on the same day. There was one cardinal rule at that establishment, the breaking of which carried the penalty of automatic expulsion, and that was that no boy could enter the building during the lunch-hour. Girls attending the commercial classes upstairs could come and go as they pleased during the break but boys had to wait outside the door until the bell rang, a rule that was strictly adhered to come hail or snow.

It was a most inclement day, the rain lashed the pavements and quickly penetrated the clothes of those who were foolish enough to turn out in the morning ill-prepared. The shelter on the lee side of the building could only accommodate so many, so the unlucky ones had to shiver and soak. Rules or no rules, two of my classmates took the chance of slipping in and concealing themselves in the toilets, but as quickly and stealthily as they moved they failed to escape the eagle eye of the caretaker. He lost no time in reporting the incident to the head, who shortly after classes had resumed summoned the two lads to his office. They returned to class a few minutes later and took their seats as if the matter had been resolved and they had suffered nothing more than a reprimand.

The teacher was standing by the blackboard, chalk in hand explaining the intricacies of English grammar when the door flew open to reveal an obviously foul-tempered headmaster.

"I've expelled those two boys. Have they gone?" he bellowed, addressing the teacher.

There was no need for the man to answer as the two lads revealed their presence by standing up and moving towards the back of the room.

"I told you two you were expelled; get out of my school," roared the head as he moved towards them with fists clenched and head lowered like a mad bull ready to attack. With only one door to the room the boys had as much chance of escaping his wrath as a couple of rats in a trap. Pupils and teacher were transfixed as if watching two gladiators about to do battle with a hungry lion. Roaring in rage and not moving too far from the door, the principal conveyed the impression he was out for blood. Fearing for their hides, the targets of his wrath moved apart and circled the room in opposite directions, going into a pincer movement that approached the head from both flanks causing him to become a little confused. Striking out wildly in both directions with fists and feet the old boy got in a couple of blows to each head and the point of a toe in one posterior before the lads made good their escape.

I was only once called upon to appear before the Great One, not because of some wrong I had done but because of a wrong I had done to me. In one of my playful moments I had rolled a piece of paper into a tight ball and using two fingers and a rubber band had flicked it at the ear of the fellow in front of me. He retaliated by turning around and splashing some ink across my face, not once but two or three times until I looked like I had broken out in a black rash. The teacher was not amused when he turned from the blackboard and noticed my speckled features.

"Very nice, I'm sure the headmaster would appreciate seeing you; just trot along and let him have a look."

My timid knock on the door was answered with a gruff request to enter. He was poring over some paperwork when I entered and didn't raise his head until I had been stood before his desk for several minutes. When he did look up he passed no remark but rose from his seat, walked to the door and, crooking his index finger, silently beckoned me to follow him. He led me down the corridor and up the stairs to the commercial classes. Opening the first door we came to he ushered me into a room full of girls and one or two lads. To an outburst of hilarious laughter he led me by the hand to the front of the class and turned me to face my audience.

"This is the type of idiot we are expected to educate downstairs; have a good look at him, I think you will find his act rather amusing."

He left the room without another word, leaving me to wriggle uncomfortably in acute embarrassment. I was on exhibition and attracting as much attention and amusement as if I were a poor man's Al Jolson about to go into a song and dance routine. Ten minutes into my ordeal the caretaker arrived to inform me that I could stand down. I didn't need to be told twice. I was out the door in a flash and before running downstairs I turned to thank my liber-ator.

"Don't thank me yet, I've got to take you on tour before you go back to your class."

He wasn't joking either. I had to suffer ten minutes making a laughing-stock of myself before every class in the school, and then I had to return to the head's office.

"You come here to learn, boy, and you have just learned one lesson. If you want to act the clown I would advise you to join a circus."

I took the admonishment to heart and tried my best to keep my nose to the grindstone and my shoulder to the wheel; alas, I was anything but a contortionist and found the strain unbearable. My good intentions died the same death as those I embraced when I had been to confession; within a few days I had kicked over the traces, only now I was clever enough not to allow myself to be caught. Embarrassment and ridicule were raiment that did not fit very comfortably and I was resolved that such attire should not cling to me again, but unfortunately it was not long before I had to suffer a similar indignity, this time because I was, among other things, a "botch".

178

THE BOTCH

However long the odds were against my becoming a business tycoon or a brain surgeon they were far shorter than my chances as a woodworker. Chippendale could rest easy in his grave, there being no chance that I would ever outdo him as a carpenter and steal any of his thunder. There are two tools associated with that trade that have always outsmarted me – the chisel and the handsaw. I have known all my life that both of these tools cease to be inanimate objects but develop wills of their own once they come into my hands. I look upon both as dangerous weapons, treating them with the same respect as I would a loaded gun, but during my tech days I had no other choice but to handle them and always with disastrous results.

Our woodwork class was run by a man who could only be described as a genius with his hands. To him even the simplest joint should be treated as a work of art, and nothing short of perfection was acceptable. He must have spent many nights in sleepless lamentations having had to spend his working days with so many who were as inept as I. The great love of his life was wood and running a close second were the tools with which to work it. Shoddy workmanship was anathema to him; he could overlook laziness, excuse tardiness or accept indifference, but for the "botch" there was no forgiveness. The strongest expletive he was ever heard to utter was the five letter word, "botch". A "botch" was the lowest form of animal life and it was the intonation he gave the word which indicated to what degree of botchery one had sunk in his estimation. I had earned the title so frequently I reckoned I should have been granted it in perpetuity in the same way as the Lonsdale Belt is awarded to a boxing champion. I was fully convinced I had earned this entitlement on the day I was relegated to the nadir of the botchery league.

The usual practice when starting a new job in the woodwork class was the issuing to each student of a couple of pieces of wood onto which each had to scribble his signature. The task allotted for this morning's work was the mortise and tenon joint. Had I been issued with a stone-age axe I could not have made a bigger mess if it: it was so bad I actually felt ashamed of it. My tenon would have passed muster as a roughly-hewn stake and the mortise looked as if it had been gnawed by a rodent with deformed incisors. I was mortified; not so much for my own ineptness but for the shock and disappointment the teacher would suffer when faced with the realisation of the futility of his calling.

Furtiveness and stealth attract attention, openness and normality pass unnoticed, so I walked purposefully across the room and opened the door to the store where was dumped an accumulation of the joinery efforts of students past and present. I heaved my abortion against the back wall, closed the door gently, walked up the room and picked up two fresh pieces of wood almost from beneath the nose of my tutor, went back to my bench and started all over again. My second effort earned me no credit but it was a masterpiece compared with what I had disposed of and had quickly forgotten.

For the remainder of the term I struggled manfully on, earning no accolades nor warranting any more brickbats than usual. On the last day before the holidays and the end of my schooldays we listened to a summary of our progress and an assessment of our future prospects as workers of wood. I was advised to take up butchery with the comment that I was more suited to wielding a cleaver than manipulating a saw. I was satisfied that I was at least considered worthy of a trade rather than condemned to a life with the pick and shovel.

There was nothing left of the session now but the clearing up; benches cleaning, floor sweeping and tool stowing, leaving the room as neat and tidy as on the first day we had entered it, ready to welcome a new generation of first-term botches. I was busily brushing down my bench when the teacher strolled up to inform me he had a special task for me. It had crossed his mind that the storeroom was over-full and in need of sorting out and would I kindly assist him? He wanted to dispose of the mediocre, retaining only those pieces that pleased his eye. Armed with the sack he had thoughtfully provided I followed him into the store. I was to have no say in what was to go or what was to stay, he being the sole arbiter and judge of what was quality and what was rubbish. Holding the sack open before me I watched and listened as he picked up the various pieces and pronounced his judgement. Every piece earned a comment before being retained or committed to banishment to the sack and eventual incineration. Not alone did he comment on each item he held in his hand but he could remember every person whose signature was inscribed on the pale wood.

"Now this boy was one of my best pupils, he had a feel for wood. I wonder what ever became of him?"

"That fellow would never make a woodworker. His parents wasted their money by sending him here."

I was almost asleep on my feet as I let the comments flow in one ear and out the other. I was only interested in hearing the bell ring to tell me I was now a man free to enter the world of the adult, leaving schools and teachers behind me.

The scream pierced my ears, stabbed my brain and almost bowled me over. For a moment I thought he had been struck by the pain of a heart attack or had his foot penetrated by a six-inch nail such was the agony of his wail. His face had turned purple as he gazed goggle-eyed at the sample of workmanship in his hands.

"You botch! You infernal botch!" he roared as he turned his gaze on me.

Thinking he had lost his reason I got ready to run, but I wasn't quick enough. He grabbed me by the collar and dragged me out to the workshop and up to his desk.

"When did you do this?" he screamed. "This never passed through my hands before, I would have destroyed it! It's a crime, an abomination; a sin against God."

He was almost in tears such was his rage, and I still had no idea what he was so upset about, not until he slapped the sin down on his desk and I saw my signature staring up and mocking me. I was a fool. I had disposed of my abomination of months before without the foresight to remove my name. I was speechless, I could only stare at him open-mouthed and, anyway, there was nothing much that I could say. Not only had I committed the unforgivable crime, I had admitted responsibility in writing; it was an open and shut case on which any jury would convict.

"I thought I had seen everything," he began, "but this takes the cake."

He lifted the object of his disgust with forefinger and thumb and held it at arm's length as if fearing contamination. I felt myself shrivel and shrink as the entire class gathered around to gawp and giggle.

"In all my years I have never seen such sacrilege," the distraught man continued. "But what really disturbs me is that the culprit had the temerity to leave his signature on it, adding insult to unforgivable injury. It grieves me to think . . ."

The sound of the bell cut him off in mid-sentence, announcing the end of term and heralding an ignominious end to my scholastic career.

The Leaving

WHEN I STEPPED out that school door for the last time I felt like a man who had just been released after a long stretch of penal servitude. What I did not realise was that leaving school without a job to go to was to wind up in limbo. It took a few weeks for me to grasp the fact that I was living in a betwixt and between world. As much as I hated schools and all that they stood for at least they gave me a reason for getting out of bed in the morning; a purpose in life, however distasteful. Now that there was nothing, time was hanging heavily and becoming an enemy. With most of my friends gone back to school or having landed some sort of job, I and a few like me kicked our heels and wandered around like lost souls.

Job applications were fruitless, not that there were many for which one could apply. It was a period of heavy unemployment and for every vacancy one got wind of there was a stampede of hopefuls, the successful candidate always being the one who had the backing of the most influential string-puller. In those days Old Nick would have been more likely to have taken Holy Orders than an egghead to secure a job in competition against a Simple Simon with the right connections. Ability or intelligence counted for nothing in a town where the political hack was king.

Like the man who complained so bitterly because he had no boots until the day he came across the fellow with

183

no feet, I cursed my luck in not being fortunate enough to find gainful employment until I realised that I was not as badly off as some of my friends. I still had my Sunday job at Murphy's and I was frequently called in during the week to help out with bottling and other little jobs associated with the trade. The remuneration didn't permit me to live the kind of life to which Riley was accustomed but it did keep the wolf at bay and provided the necessities of life like cigarettes, pictures and the odd visit to a hop. When it came to chasing after the girls I was out of the running: it was not that I was an oddball, but I could never catch one who was willing to pick up the tab for a night on the town.

Murphy's became a second home to me; I wandered in and out at will like a stray cat that had once been offered a saucer of milk and couldn't be got rid of. I never drew any pay for my uninvited visits but it kept me off the streets and out of what was termed "bad company". Though there was temptation in abundance I never did get around to imbibing as my earlier experience with the effects of cider had frightened me off all alcoholic beverages. For the student of human nature I would say there is no better university than to serve behind the bar of a public house. Nothing short of brain transplantation could have a quicker or more dramatic effect on a man's personality than a few shots of alcohol. To see a great hulk of brawn and muscle reduced to a babbling, incoherent softie after a few pints never ceased to amaze me; or the meek little nondescript suddenly deluding himself into thinking he was ten feet tall and wanting to fight everybody in the house would both frighten and baffle me. I was never able to figure out how one man could sit and drink all day and walk out seemingly as sober as a judge and how another character would come in, get a sniff of a cork, and have to be forcibly ejected as drunk as a lord.

There was nothing to be gained from hanging around pondering on the follies of the feckless and when an

184

acquaintance informed me that he could fix me up with a temporary job I jumped at the chance. It was for the Electricity Board, out in the country painting pylons; the pay was good according to the standards of the day and would keep me going throughout the summer. I bade farewell to Mrs Murphy and her pub, bought myself a pair of overalls, and on Monday set off on the first leg of a lifetime's labour.

The line to be painted ran all the way to the county of Limerick, and would at least satisfy my desire for other vistas. Our transport was the same as that which had taken me on that ill-fated trip to the bog in an earlier summer, but this time our employers were considerate enough to fit it out with a tarpaulin cover as protection against the elements. We were to work in pairs, two men to each pylon, and we were miles from town before my partner and I were set down armed with paint, wire brushes and chipping hammers to make our way across the corn-fields and meadows to our objective.

One of the pleasures of my boyhood was tree-climbing so it was with some surprise that I found myself suffering from a sudden attack of vertigo. I was gripped by a terror I had never known. I had climbed up easily enough but when I looked down and saw that there were no leafy branches between me and eternity I froze to the ironwork. My companion tried his best to reassure me but he was wasting his breath; I would rather have faced every demon in hell than relax my grip. A voice inside whispered that I was too young to die but I refused to believe it and seriously thought of hurling myself into space and to destruction rather than prolong the agony. My mate did all sorts of gymnastics to try to convince me how groundless my fears were, but it wasn't until he lost his patience and threatened to abandon me that my terror departed as quickly as it had overcome me, never more to return.

For refreshment we had brought sandwiches, tea, sugar

and milk, with a kettle in which to brew. As a novice on the job I was delegated the position of catering manager and despatched to the nearest farmhouse to procure a boiling of water. I was to learn that farmers and their kin were not the tight-fisted skinflints that they were generally labelled. The first woman I approached would not hear of us sitting out in her yard feeding on nothing more substantial than cheese sandwiches, but insisted that we come in, sit at the table and stuff ourselves on bacon, cabbage and potatoes, washed down by large mugs of strong hot tea. It was hospitality that we were to find all along the line with only a few exceptions. By the time we had worked our way to the end of the job my views on the rustic world were drastically changed; I had learned the lesson that kindness and generosity are not the monopoly of any one community, but that wherever we belong we are all brothers underneath the skin.

Summer was halfway through and we were starting out on the final run down the line; soon the job would be completed and I would once again be unemployed. It was time to be making plans to build a more secure future. It was a time of mass migration; young men and women were packing their utility suitcases and departing from the scene every day of the week. Familiar faces were vanishing overnight: it was as if a plague were sweeping through the town, carrying off the young and healthy. Hardly an evening went by in which I did not bump into some friend who did not stop to inform me that he was catching the first train out in the morning, bound for the emigrant boat and Birmingham or London. I found a sadness in the farewells because though brave faces were shown I would detect an underlying reluctance to take that vital step. I felt that if I did not join the exodus I would wind up like a Robinson Crusoe, alone, cut off from my own generation, a castaway in a denuded nation.

My father had been working in London for several years

and on his last visit home had invited me to come and join
him even if it were to be only for a holiday. I had saved a
few quid while working on the power lines and figured
that there would be no better time to take the plunge. My
first step was to have my photo taken and then to go to the
Guards' barracks to complete the other formalities
required to qualify for a travel permit card, or what we
mistakenly called a passport. I was going to pull up my
roots and depart exactly one week after my temporary job
came to an end. I told my boss of my plans and he looked
upon them with disfavour. To him there was no place like
home and he did his best to convince me that I had made a
wrong decision. He went so far as to suggest that if I could
manage to ride out the winter he would do all he could to
get me employed on a permanent basis. I rejected his kind
offer in my innocent belief that faraway hills were green
and that foreign streets were paved with gold.

As the date of my departure drew closer I was filled
with a mixture of excitement and trepidation; having
assured family and friends that there would be no turning
chicken, inwardly I was tormented by doubt. Although
England was our nearest neighbour it was still a foreign
land with a different life style and culture. I had heard
many glowing reports from those who swore they would
never again settle down in Ireland, but there were also
those for whom it would ever be an alien environment to
which they could never adjust. I pondered long and hard
on how I would cope with the contrast between a small
town and the world's largest city.

I wandered around and surveyed my neighbourhood
with a keener eye: in the decade or so that had passed
since our young gang had ruled the roost changes had
occurred that I had never noticed before. A new gang
played ball in the street but they were better attired than
we had ever been, and they had a real ball rather than the
bundle of rags tied up with string with which we had to

make do. Our old swimming pools had fallen out of favour, the dams we had kept in such good repair had now disintegrated for want of maintenance and trout would have difficulty in navigating where we once stood waist-deep in the cooling water. The field with the buttercups and daisies where the milkmaids once frolicked was now a council tip and the banks that were home to cowslip and primrose looked set to vanish beneath the rubbish and waste of urban sprawl. Downriver I made my way to the pool where Rose had met her miserable and lonely end, but of her or the rock that had anchored her to her final bed there was no trace; time and tide had washed all away leaving nothing but the memory.

The sun came out to smile on me that September morning when I left the house on my way to the station. I had said my goodbyes at home. I knew that there would be enough tears washing around to swill the departure platform without me and mine adding to the deluge. It was easy to pick out the hardened travellers from the firsttimers; the smiling groups contrasted strongly with those that were providing the water-works. I found myself a seat with my back to the engine and consoled myself by watching the performances on the platform: the weeping and wailing as if the departing were going to the grave rather than to a new life, the hugs and handshakes that threatened to cause serious physical damage to the recipients, and the loud keening that would warrant a round of applause at any good wake.

I sighed with relief when the whistle blew and the engine groaned to send out a blast of steam that wafted down the platform, mercifully shrouding the mourners from view. A few loud chugs and a slight jerk took us gently out of the station, beyond the level crossing and out into the country. Foley's glen and the track over the top of Slieve Mish stood out sharply in the early morning sunlight and as we gathered speed they slowly vanished from view. The familiar outline of the mountain began to alter by the minute and before I realised it I was viewing it from the other side. Like a giant purple curtain it had drawn across to shut out the valley in which I had been born and nurtured, and which was now being left behind like the nest from which the young bird departs.

Yale R. 70

Morbet Salin